THE
ASSISTANT
PRINCIPAL
IDENTITY

ALSO BY BARUTI K. KAFELE

The Equity and Social Justice Education 50:
Critical Questions for Improving Opportunities
and Outcomes for Black Students

The Assistant Principal 50:
Critical Questions for Meaningful Leadership and Professional Growth

The Aspiring Principal 50:
Critical Questions for New and Future School Leaders

Is My School a Better School Because I Lead It?

The Teacher 50:
Critical Questions for Inspiring Classroom Excellence

The Principal 50:
Critical Leadership Questions for Inspiring Schoolwide Excellence

Closing the Attitude Gap:
How to Fire Up Your Students to Strive for Success

Motivating Black Males to Achieve in School and in Life

THE
ASSISTANT
PRINCIPAL
IDENTITY

Protecting Your Leadership Mindset, Fervor, and Authenticity

BARUTI K. KAFELE

Arlington, Virginia USA

2800 Shirlington Road, Suite 1001 • Arlington, VA 22206 USA
Phone: 800-933-2723 or 703-578-9600 • Fax: 703-575-5400
Website: www.ascd.org • Email: member@ascd.org
Author guidelines: www.ascd.org/write

Penny Reinart, *Deputy Executive Director;* Genny Ostertag, *Managing Director, Book Acquisitions & Editing;* Mary Beth Nielsen, *Director, Book Editing;* Liz Wegner, *Editor;* Thomas Lytle, *Creative Director;* Donald Ely, *Art Director;* Lisa Hill, *Graphic Designer;* Cynthia Stock, *Typesetter;* Kelly Marshall, *Production Manager;* Shajuan Martin, *E-Publishing Specialist;* Christopher Logan, *Senior Production Specialist*

All web links in this book are correct as of the publication date below but may have become inactive or otherwise modified since that time. If you notice a deactivated or changed link, please email books@ascd.org with the words "Link Update" in the subject line. In your message, please specify the web link, the book title, and the page number on which the link appears.

PAPERBACK ISBN: 978-1-4166-3226-9   ASCD product #123049   n5/23
PDF EBOOK ISBN: 978-1-4166-3227-6; see Books in Print for other formats.
Quantity discounts are available: email programteam@ascd.org or call 800-933-2723, ext. 5773, or 703-575-5773. For desk copies, go to www.ascd.org/deskcopy.

Library of Congress Cataloging-in-Publication Data

Names: Kafele, Baruti K., author.
Title: The assistant principal identity : protecting your leadership mindset, fervor, and authenticity / Baruti K. Kafele.
Description: Arlington, VA : ASCD, [2023] | Includes bibliographical references and index.
Identifiers: LCCN 2023001049 (print) | LCCN 2023001050 (ebook) | ISBN 9781416632269 (paperback) | ISBN 9781416632276 (pdf)
Subjects: LCSH: Assistant school principals—United States. | Educational leadership—United States. | School management and organization—United States.
Classification: LCC LB2831.92 .K3394 2023 (print) | LCC LB2831.92 (ebook) | DDC 371.2/012—dc23/eng/20230120
LC record available at https://lccn.loc.gov/2023001049
LC ebook record available at https://lccn.loc.gov/2023001050

32 31 30 29 28 27 26 25 24 23   1 2 3 4 5 6 7 8 9 10 11 12

The Assistant Principal Identity *is dedicated to my entire Virtual AP Leadership Academy family. We started together the first Saturday of May 2020 and have been going strong ever since with no ending in sight. Your consistent participation and engagement keep me inspired and encouraged about not only your roles as assistant principals but the principalships that each of you will step into along your leadership journey.*

THE ASSISTANT PRINCIPAL IDENTITY

Introduction

For many years, I have had a near obsession with the role of the assistant principal. I have felt for more than two decades that the assistant principalship is the most misunderstood and underutilized position in all of education. As I travel the country, the number of assistant principals in urban, suburban, and rural schools who spend entire days disciplining children is staggering. As I've said repeatedly, excessive discipline problems are the manifestation of a school and classroom culture that requires maximum attention. Although there are challenges in homes, neighborhoods, and communities that manifest in schools, those challenges don't have to be reflected in schools. Schools can be the oases from the challenges of the world outside the school, as well as sources of hope and possibility for students.

I can't state enough that the role of the assistant principal (AP) is significant in all aspects of school leadership. The assistant principal is critical to the success of a school. The person in this role cannot be relegated to a full-time school disciplinarian because there are too many other aspects of the work of school leadership in which the assistant principal must be inherently engaged, starting with instructional leadership. Take, for example, an assistant principal who supervises 20 teachers in a low-performing school. That the school is low performing warrants that the assistant principal provide teachers with maximum attention, including ongoing coaching and observation. If disciplining students interferes with the AP being the coach that the teachers require, chances are that this school will continue to be a low-performing one—because of the priorities of the overall leadership (inclusive of the principal) of the school, *not* because of ineffective leadership. The overall culture of the school must be a priority of the leadership so that the school functions as the leadership envisions it can.

Additionally, the assistant principal must be continuously coached by the principal. It is a given that there are assistant principals who have absolutely *no* desire to become principals, and that's OK (as many are much more effective in the assistant's role than they would be as principals). Be that as it may, the AP still needs ongoing coaching to become the best possible assistant principal. The reality in far too many instances is that a teacher or a counselor will interview for the position of assistant principal, land the position, and be immediately relegated to disciplinarian, lunch duty, or bus duty. My question then is, what about all of the other responsibilities of being an effective school leader and, in this instance, an effective assistant principal?

In 2019, I wrote a blog post entitled "The Assistant Principalship: The Most Misunderstood and Underutilized Position in Education." I had no real expectation regarding the views it would garner as it was one of a long line of blog posts I had written over the years. To my surprise, it went viral. I couldn't believe the number of people who took an interest in it and with whom it resonated. It spoke volumes to me because the content was comparable to what I have written here thus far. And then when the feedback started coming in, I knew my contentions about the role of the AP were spot on. A large number of frustrated assistant principals reached out to me and shared their frustrations about serving as full-time disciplinarians. (I often remind educators and noneducators alike that countless assistant principals were outstanding teachers and counselors before they ventured into school leadership.) Countless adults are successful because of their teachers and counselors. In other words, we're talking about some very talented educators who, all of a sudden, are in positions in which the talents that got them there are now underutilized. This must change.

As a follow-up to the aforementioned blog post, I wrote *The Assistant Principal 50* (2020). It resonated with tens of thousands of aspiring and current assistant principals and quickly became an ASCD bestseller. But I didn't stop there. In May 2020, I launched the Virtual AP Leadership Academy—a live stream event that takes place every Saturday morning on YouTube, Twitter, and Facebook—where I coach aspiring and current assistant principals or interview guests. But I didn't stop there either. In 2021, I created the Virtual AP Leadership Academy Facebook page; it's devoted to assistant principals and is where, every Sunday morning, I write a commentary to aspiring and current assistant principals toward the end of coaching them weekly as a follow-up to the Saturday Virtual AP Leadership Academy.

In short, I am committed to the professional growth, development, and evolution of the assistant principal. In addition to classroom and school equity, the assistant principalship is my primary area of focus. I believe with every fiber of my being that this role can be transformed in schools where the assistant principal's exposure is limited and the role is reduced to disciplinarian, lunch duty, bus duty, and the like.

The Purpose of This Book

In my Virtual AP Leadership Academy, before I get to my main topic, the motivator in me starts off with an uplifting message—a commentary to get things started. Somewhere along the way, a theme evolved wherein, for about 30 weeks, I prefaced each message with the word *protecting* (e.g., protecting your truth, protecting your peace, protecting your worth, protecting your commitment, protecting your happiness, protecting your attitude). I'd exclaim to my audience, for example, "You've got to protect your *happiness* the same way you protect your loved ones, property, possessions, and job, because your happiness is a key ingredient to your effectiveness as a school leader."

Let's go further with this. Educators receive professional development training relative to their roles throughout their careers via in-service training, conferences, institutes, academies, coaching, dialoguing with other professionals, videos, live streams, podcasts, books, journals, blogs, and social media. The goal is ongoing professional growth and development toward becoming a more competent and effective school leader. As I pondered this over the years, I concluded that yes, professional growth and development matter immensely. However, due to the complexities of the work, it is easy—very easy—for gains made to diminish. In fact, it is easy to lose *yourself* in this field if you're not careful. It's comparable to learning a foreign language—if you're not disciplined and don't retain and use what you learned, you'll lose it in a very short period of time. Gains must therefore be protected, and this protection comes in the form of consistently using what was learned while simultaneously striving to become better and better in any given area of leadership.

As I will get into in depth in this book, school leadership is quite complex and has many moving parts—visible and invisible, tangible and intangible—and no two days are alike. The aforementioned characteristics that must be protected (e.g., truth, peace, worth, happiness) can be compromised.

I considered the characteristics, qualities, attributes, traits, values—ingredients, as it were—associated with assistant principals. Although I initially came up with 30, I knew there were so many more that were pertinent to an assistant principal's effectiveness. Therefore, I generated a comprehensive list of 105 ingredients: 35 that will be addressed in this book, 35 in a second book, and 35 in a third book. My premise is that all of them are absolutely vital to an AP's, or any leader's, overall effectiveness. Although these ingredients may already be or become a part of your current leadership identity, you must intentionally and vigilantly protect each of them from being compromised or violated. Allowing just one of the 35 in this book to be compromised can severely undermine your leadership effectiveness (e.g., if your truth is compromised, your overall leadership effectiveness can be compromised). You must therefore be vigilant about protecting all that I will share with you in this book.

I am well aware of how "protecting" is viewed in the professional learning world of school leadership. Typically, when we talk about professional learning, we're talking about professional growth and professional development, which makes sense. However, after years of observing colleagues in leadership roles at all levels encounter the wide array of challenges and the adverse impact that they had or could have on a leader, I began to ask myself the following three questions:

> » How can school leaders *protect themselves* from being compromised during challenging and difficult times?

> » How can school leaders *protect their leadership* from being compromised during challenging and difficult times?

> » How can school leaders *protect their professional gains* from being compromised during challenging and difficult times?

These are very different questions from those that focus on professional growth and development, which are centered around how leaders can get better, become more effective, or sharpen their skills. *This book centers around how leaders can maintain, sustain, and protect themselves, their leadership, and their professional gains in the midst of challenging times.* Because I have witnessed for decades with my own eyes leaders who have struggled with protecting themselves and the components of their leadership, and because I have devoted my professional life to assistant principal development, this book contains 35 self-reflective questions and accompanying commentaries divided into the following three chapters:

» Protecting my leadership mindset

» Protecting my leadership fervor

» Protecting my leadership authenticity

Collectively, I look at leadership mindset, fervor, and authenticity as key components of the assistant principal's overall leadership identity. The assistant principal identity asks the self-reflective question, "Who am I as assistant principal?" The answer to this question is critical to how assistant principals see themselves, how assistant principals are being perceived by those they lead, who the assistant principals actually are as leaders, and the assistant principals' overall mission and purpose for leading. In this book, I want assistant principals to look deeply within themselves toward not only discovering and establishing a leadership identity but also growing and cultivating a leadership identity that is constantly evolving throughout their leadership journey. As the title of this book suggests, the identity of the assistant principal is an important aspect of the assistant principal's overall leadership, and it is rooted in the assistant principal's mindset, fervor, and authenticity.

With the goal of making this book highly relatable and authentic—having served as a school leader for 14 years, teacher for 7 years, and public speaker for the past 37 years—each self-reflective question will begin with a personal account that describes an experience that I had as an assistant principal, a principal, a teacher, or a speaker/consultant. Many educators want to know about my personal experiences in the classroom and as a school leader, so these 35 vignettes will bring readers into my professional world and allow you to see how I approached each situation posed in the question. I will then discuss you and your leadership within each question by asking, "What about *you?*" Throughout the book, I will simultaneously speak to you as an assistant principal and one who is preparing for the principalship. As always, I will be speaking directly to you.

As is the case with all of my books, this book is not meant to be read once and put aside. I encourage you to reference it regularly, use it as a mirror, and consider it a companion to *The Assistant Principal 50.*

CHAPTER 1

Protecting My Leadership Mindset

n all things related to school leadership and, specifically, assistant principal leadership, I can think of nothing more significant than the state of mind of the leader. Everything, and I mean *everything*, starts there—not with your skill set, which is derived from your mindset. *Your mindset is the foundation to your leadership and pretty much everything in life.* For example, I began writing this book in August—the month in which I spoke in a different city and state every day. I could have easily justified not writing a book during that month. However, my mindset let me know that I could handle it. In fact, my mindset said to me, "Let's get it done! Let's make it happen! No time to procrastinate! No time is an ideal time! Now is the time!" Interestingly, though, that wasn't always my mindset; it evolved through growth and development. Eventually, I had to protect it. And because I protected my mindset, it's now habitual for me to be self-accountable and not let anything or anyone prevent me from meeting my objectives or pursuing my goals, aspirations, and dreams.

Let's now break down protecting the assistant principal leadership mindset.

Q1 How am I protecting my leadership *attitude?*

I had a brief year-and-a-half stint as an assistant principal that I consider the lowest point of my professional career. Why? Because I learned little about school leadership and was reduced to being a disciplinarian. I went into that position with an overwhelmingly positive attitude and was eager to assist with taking children to their next levels. One year before becoming an assistant principal, I was named the Teacher of the Year at the school, district, and county levels and was a finalist for New Jersey State Teacher of the Year. Shortly thereafter, I was appointed assistant principal at a neighboring school in the same district, and I took that Teacher of the Year energy with me. I soon learned that the credentials I brought along didn't translate into a comparable experience. Being a disciplinarian—which included regularly dealing with angry parents, lunch duty, and bus duty and serving as supply/inventory clerk—wasn't exactly rewarding on the heels of my classroom experience. But you know something? My attitude was protected; it was under lock and key and safe from harm. In other words, I knew there was more to me (and I never forgot that), and I knew that my best days were ahead of me. I knew that my current circumstances didn't define my possibilities, potential, or capacity to lead at a high level. I was convinced, through my attitude, that my situation was temporary and that all I worked for would soon be realized.

A year later, I was appointed principal of the same school. I had protected my attitude from being compromised by intentionally being positive and optimistic throughout the year. I didn't allow my situation or the associated distractions to get the better of me. I didn't allow pessimism, frustration, or disgust into my psyche. I conditioned my mind into believing that better days were ahead while never losing sight of the reason I entered this profession—my *why*.

What about *you*?

Your attitude is your state of mind—which, as an assistant principal, is crucial to your overall success as one of the leaders of your school. Everything you do as a school leader begins with your attitude. As the saying goes, your attitude will determine your altitude. And remember that whatever skill set you develop over time is rooted in your attitude, which is *everything*.

Is your current situation as an assistant principal good, favorable, or rewarding? Is it less than you expected? Is it discouraging or frustrating? Do you feel that you're being underutilized or mis-used? Are you being overlooked or virtually ignored? Is your situation diminishing your desire to one day become a princi-pal? Does it have you considering returning to the classroom?

These questions have everything to do with your attitude in the midst of a bad or less-than-rewarding situation. If you by chance find yourself in a situation comparable to the one I found myself in, my question to you is, how are you preventing your attitude from being compromised? That is, how are you protecting your attitude from . . . you? This is the hand that was dealt to you. It doesn't mean that you don't have influence (which I will discuss in Chapter 3). You have to deal with your current reality without losing your spirit. You must safeguard—protect—the positive attitude that you brought to this position and the goal of one day becoming a highly effective principal. How? Constantly remind yourself why you pursued an admin-istrative position in the first place. You can never, ever lose sight of your why (i.e., your purpose), which must rest at the heart and soul of your attitude. It can never be lost or misplaced. It is too critical to your forward progress. Your why is your attitude protection. It serves as your mirror for continual self-reflection and self-assessment. As the work in whatever situation becomes increasingly challenging, you can never lose sight as to why you got into this work in the first place and where it is you expect to go. This is your purpose. Keeping your why close to the vest increases the probability that your attitude toward the work will be protected, regardless of your circumstances.

Q2 How am I protecting my leadership *purpose*?

When I think of my why, I can vividly recall a trip to Newark Liberty International Airport in my home state of New Jersey. I was scheduled to fly to New Orleans to deliver a keynote address to about 4,000 registrants, so I was really excited about the opportunity. When I got to the TSA agent and opened my wallet to retrieve my driver's license, to my shock and dismay, it was not there. I immediately recalled where it was (on the glass of my home copier). I begged and pleaded with the agent to let me through, to no avail. I left that airport like a puppy with its tail between its legs. Dejected, disgusted, and disappointed, I was reluctant to call the client to relay that I would not be delivering the keynote address at an event that had been planned a year in advance! As I drove back home to Jersey City, I reached a conclusion that has guided my practice ever since—leaving home without your why is equivalent to leaving home without your ID. There will be no flying . . . that day.

What about *you*?

Why did you choose leadership? When it hit you that you wanted to be an assistant principal and, subsequently, a school leader, what did you want to accomplish? Of all the things that you want to accomplish as a school leader, what's that one thing that you must accomplish to make your leadership complete? That one thing is more than likely your *why*. As critically important as your why is to your leadership, how you protect it is more important. That is, knowing your why may not necessarily translate into it being easy or straightforward to walk in.

Depending on the complexity of your why, it could be a career-long pursuit that is never definitively achieved, which is OK as long as progress is being made along the journey and you are passionate about the process. What's key here, though, is that you keep your why under lock and key—fully protected. This means that although the challenges are ongoing, you can never, ever allow yourself to feel so defeated and deflated that you abandon your why—your reason for leading, your purpose, your *because*. That means you must approach your why with fervor to ensure that it is protected through whatever may come.

If you lose your why, you lose your way—and your will along with it. When you lose your will, your why gets reduced to your work or a job—something that, in your capacity as a leader, you never, ever want to happen.

Q3 How am I protecting my leadership *confidence?*

Several years ago, I was invited to speak at a weekend teachers' retreat. My charge was to deliver a one-hour keynote address on Friday evening and conduct a three-hour workshop on Saturday afternoon. For whatever reason, it was clear to me that my keynote address was not a hit. I didn't feel the connection with the audience at all. Although it was difficult for me to gauge why the connection wasn't there, I attributed it in part to the fact that it was a Friday evening and I was speaking to an audience of teachers who were likely drained after teaching all day. Moreover, for the rest of the evening, I personalized what I deemed defeat and didn't feel that I could go into the workshop confidently the following day, which bothered me deeply. In less than 24 hours, I had to face the same audience twice. In my mind, my reputation and my brand as a speaker were on the line. I had to quickly come up with a strategy to bounce back.

Clearly, I did not protect my confidence. I allowed myself to feel defeated. My decades of experience didn't matter to me at that time. The only thing that mattered was that I failed to deliver. My confidence in myself as a presenter was compromised. When I got back to my hotel room, I began the process of rebuilding myself. I reminded myself of all of the work I had done as a presenter for two decades, that I was there because someone invited me predicated on my previous work, that I was a professional, and that my message adds value. In doing that, I was rebuilding and restoring my self-confidence. I soon after turned in for the night and woke up before sunrise to prepare in the morning. (I've never prepared for a presentation as long as I prepared for that one—a total of eight hours!) I was not going to be defeated a second time. I was ready, and my confidence was now restored and protected. I knew I was ready, and I knew my worth to that audience—and I now knew the audience. I anticipated a standing ovation, which, along with cheers, I received! It took that experience to remind me that when I fall, there's nothing wrong about owning the fall. However, my confidence in my abilities, which must be protected and rooted in past experiences and successes, can never be compromised.

What about *you*?

Let me tell you something, assistant principal: all days are not going to be your best days. All days are not going to be good days. In your role as assistant principal, there are going to be some days that will in fact force you to question whether school leadership is how you want to spend the rest of your professional life. But there will be other days when you are convinced that you are walking in your purpose. It all balances out. But on those bad or not-so-good days (or even weeks) when nothing seems to be going right and your confidence appears to be waning, what do you have in place that reminds you of who and what you are? What do you have in place that reminds you of what you have already accomplished to get you where you are? What do you have in place that reminds you that you matter? What do you have in place that reminds you that you add value? Your confidence cannot be sustained through professional learning alone. Your confidence must be protected, and you must be intentional about protecting your confidence in yourself and your leadership at all costs. It is simply not realistic to believe that you can lead at a high level of effectiveness when you lack confidence in doing so. Your confidence must be restored when it wanes. You must regularly remind yourself that you are qualified to be in this position or it wouldn't have been offered to you. It is so easy for a leader to become mired in tough situations and not bounce back quickly. Imagine a staff meeting where you had an agenda item that became such an emotional hot topic that staff came at you individually with questions and concerns that you had not anticipated and couldn't answer intelligently. You leave the meeting feeling so defeated you don't feel that you can adequately facilitate the next staff meeting. You must not allow yourself to get to this point. In this scenario, you must anticipate the fallout and be thoroughly prepared for all possible questions and concerns that may arise. It's all in the preparation. As an assistant principal, you must always protect your confidence in your leadership.

Q4 How am I protecting my leadership *drive* and *determination*?

As a classroom teacher, an assistant principal, and a principal, I was "hungry." I probably wanted more for my students than they wanted for themselves. Their success was personal to me. The story of my high school years is widely known. (I attended four high schools and graduated in five years with a grade point average of 1.5. I was in bad shape.) The five years that followed (which I refer to as "my five years of nothingness") were even more disastrous. After those 10 years, in an effort to make something of myself, I enrolled at Kean University and went on to graduate summa cum laude, which shows that my potential had been lying dormant and that no one at the grade-school level had been able to activate it. Those years at Kean were personal, and I wanted to prove to myself and everyone around me what I was capable of achieving. My newfound drive and determination, which emanated from my newfound attitude and confidence, were highly personal.

I took this spirit into the classroom and, subsequently, into school leadership. The success of my students was *personal*. I never saw my leadership role as a job, career, or profession. It was always personal and just happened to exist in a professional setting. I often yell to my audiences during keynote addresses, "It's personal!" Because it was and remains so personal, the success I have been able to build and maintain over the past 35 years has allowed me to day in and day out sustain an ultra-high level of drive and determination toward being the best version of myself within my leadership role that I can be. I seldom require an alarm to awaken me in the morning, even after only three to four hours of sleep. I have always been ready and eager to start a new day. As a classroom teacher and as a principal, I was fired up about the prospects for the new day. As an assistant principal, despite the sentiments that I expressed earlier, I was fired up about the prospects and possibilities of what I felt in my bones was going to be a quick transition into the principalship; that was my confidence on full display. My drive and determination were protected in all three capacities. It was personal.

What about *you*?

Where do you get your drive and determination? Do you possess the requisite drive and determination to do your work at a high level? Are you eager to jump back into your leadership role every morning? Are you eager to lead your students to heights previously unimagined every day? Is your work in any way personal? If so, in what way and why? Or is your work strictly professional? Are your drive and determination protected?

Professional learning can't develop your drive and determination in isolation. Actually, no one can teach you drive and determination. Drive and determination have to come from within; they have to be a part of your mindset. Professional learning can, at best, tell you what drive and determination comprise. Embodying them must come from within, which is where your mirror comes into play. If you ever get to a point where you feel that you lack drive or determination, you've got to ask yourself why. As a school leader, if your drive and determination are drawn solely from the professional side of your work, that may be why they're lacking. If, on the other hand, your drive and determination are drawn from something much deeper, something personal to you, there may be more incentive for you to go harder for your staff and students every day. As you develop and sustain the sense of drive and determination, you must protect it from distractions. You've got to recall why your work is so personal. You must ask yourself, "What is that thing inside of me that screams loudly that this work must get done and at a high level?" If you lose sight of it, only a portion of you—a shell of yourself and not your full essence—is leading. Your students and staff need your leadership drive and determination to lead them to the next level of accomplishment, so protect them.

Q5 How am I protecting my leadership enthusiasm?

In my fourth year as a 5th grade teacher, my superintendent at the time decided to departmentalize the elementary schools beginning at grade 3. He felt that teachers would perform more effectively if they were given the opportunity to focus on that one content area about which they were passionate, which worked for me. I loved social studies, and now I could teach it all day. This was the first time that our students were changing classrooms. The 5th grade students were the oldest in the building—and the loudest in the hallway during the change of classes. Although my 5th grade colleagues and I really thought we had a handle on the talking between classes, the principal felt otherwise. She convened a meeting of the 5th grade teachers and emphatically stated, "Beginning tomorrow, the students will remain in their classrooms and the teachers will change classes." Yikes! This meant that I would teach in four different classrooms. Understand that a great deal of my enthusiasm stemmed from the way I celebrated my students through the usage of my walls (which contained photos of my students, student awards, pictures and posters of historical figures, work samples, motivational quotes, and student marking period goals).

There are many days throughout my 21 years in education before becoming a speaker and consultant that I don't remember, but I remember that day vividly. During the meeting, I recall informing the principal of the significance of the classroom environment I created and how it greatly contributed to the overall climate and culture of my classroom. I told her emphatically that, for that reason, I couldn't be effective in another teacher's classroom. Her response to me was, "Kafele, I suggest you take that classroom and strap it to your back and bring it with you, because you will be changing classes tomorrow." Ouch!

In that moment, my enthusiasm for my work was completely gone. I wanted to quit my job. I devoted a great deal of time and energy into creating a certain classroom environment—commencing work a month before school started! I felt deflated, almost broken. How was I going to be able to teach in another teacher's space? Well, because I knew something about people skills from my marketing days in undergraduate school and immediately following graduation, I concluded it was time to use them to the fullest. I met with my principal alone after the meeting. I convinced her that both I and the students would be placed at a disadvantage if I were made to change classrooms, that the classroom was my Superman cape, and that the students would be taught by a teacher whose cape had been taken away and was not at full strength. She replied, "Kafele, you better go to your team and tell them if I hear one sound up there, the teachers are going back to changing classes." No sounds were ever heard in the hallways again.

In this scenario, I protected my enthusiasm. My enthusiasm had been temporarily compromised and, had I not acted quickly, it could have been compromised for an extended period of time. I had to examine the situation and determine how I was going to revive my enthusiasm, and the solution was to use my people skills.

What about *you*?

As an assistant principal, you are in a position that I have described to countless school leaders over the past several years as "the most misunderstood and underutilized position in all of education." I find that it never quite looks the same in different schools. The common denominator, however, is the large number of assistant principals who serve as full-time disciplinarians, particularly in urban and rural schools. Although this is a reality for many, it would be difficult for me to imagine that becoming a full-time disciplinarian was the driving force behind pursuing a position as a school leader. I would think that most of us wanted to come into this role to create magic for young people. When an assistant principal has been relegated to serving primarily as disciplinarian and must be on duty during lunch and be on bus duty when students arrive and leave school for the day, it's inevitable that enthusiasm will take a real hit. So my question then would be, what are you doing to protect your enthusiasm? But I could also go on to ask, did you bring a high level of enthusiasm with you to your assignment in the first place? If so, what was the root of your enthusiasm? Was it personal or solely professional? Did it drive you thus far? Does it still matter to you? Are you fully committed to it?

Your enthusiasm is fragile; it can be strong in one moment and shatter and break the next (if you allow it to). Therefore, you must safeguard it, protect it. Just as I tapped into my people skills when dealing with my principal, if you find yourself in a situation where you can't shift your reality without the aid of your principal, you might have to reach into your people skills bag to let your principal know that there is more to you than your current assignment(s). That is, you must protect your enthusiasm by being strategic in your reaction to a situation that compromises your enthusiasm.

Looked at differently and again using the example of an assistant principal serving as a full-time disciplinarian, perhaps your time is being greatly misused (i.e., you are a full-time disciplinarian because the overall culture of your school is steeped in toxicity, translating to you expending unnecessary energy in all of the wrong places). Through an earnest assessment of your current reality, for example, you have determined that the culture of the school, not student behavior, is the root of the problem. As you reach this conclusion and shift your focus, you discover that there's no need to spend all day on disciplinary referrals and instead turn your attention to addressing the culture of the school which, in the long run, frees you up to engage in aspects of the school that are meaningful and fulfilling. You now once again feel that you matter and hence, you have protected your enthusiasm for your work.

Q6 How am I protecting my leadership urgency?

I recall one year during my principalship when we set our state assessment goals quite high based on what we'd achieved the previous year (which was slightly more than we'd achieved the year prior). Although we were considered a low-performing school, I felt strongly that my students were in the right school with the right staff and leadership. I desperately wanted to show the world what my students—in an urban school district that was predominantly African American with a free and reduced lunch rate of about 85 percent and where crime, gangs, and drugs were ever present—were capable of achieving. I urgently wanted to demonstrate that we could beat the odds. I was raised in that same city and beat those same odds, so I knew that my students could do so as well. We worked diligently all year long to turn our vision into our reality. I termed our work as urgent. I felt that if we could make it happen for our students, we could be a model for schools with similar demographics across the country.

Well, at the end of the year, the assessment scores were released, and we had a setback. Our scores dropped. I felt empty and questioned whether I was built for school leadership. My sense of urgency was lost because, in my mind, I had given that school all that I had. My direct supervisor called me into his office and asked me what happened. I proceeded to tell him how hard I had worked throughout the year. He told me that he was aware of how hard I had worked but questioned how smart I had worked. That stung! It took me about two weeks to recover emotionally from it. When I did, I made significant shifts in how I prepared for the new school year and how I led throughout the year. I was still a leadership newbie and had a lot to learn. In making various adjustments to my preparation (e.g., better strategic planning) and to my overall leadership throughout the year, I regained my sense of urgency. I vowed to never again allow an experience or someone's words to compromise my sense of urgency. I could now go hard again for my students while protecting my urgency. Regardless of successes or setbacks, I refused to allow anything or anyone to deter me from my mission of showing the world what urban Black children living in economically disadvantaged communities could achieve when they are surrounded by staff and leadership who demonstrate a sense of urgency.

What about *you*?

When you think about your leadership, what have you deemed urgent? What components of your leadership are nonnegotiable? What's that thing that keeps you up at night that you must accomplish? What's that thing that eats away at your soul and dominates your thinking and has inspired you to say, "I won't stop, I won't rest until this thing is completed?" What's that thing that makes you proclaim, "Nothing and no one will interfere with me achieving this objective?" What aspects of your work do you consider urgent? I am also asking you how you are protecting your sense of urgency, because it can be compromised if you fail to protect it.

Yes, you have chosen a challenging field (the most challenging, I dare say) in which to lead. In most leadership endeavors, adults are leading adults. However, in K–12 education, adults simultaneously lead adults and children—which requires two very different leadership skills. Although leading children has little in common with leading adults, school leaders are required and expected to be proficient at leading both. Given the two leadership skills required, in what regard do you feel a sense of urgency? I have been known to say publicly for the past couple of decades that the biggest crisis and challenge in education is the crisis and challenge of the Black male learner. This is not to say that the Black male learner is the problem, though. It's to say that, as a national system of education, we have not to date figured out how to connect with and properly educate and empower the Black male learner. In this regard, as a Black man, I felt a strong sense of urgency toward my Black male students. But given the duality of school leadership, I led them in one regard while also effectively leading my staff toward competently motivating, educating, and empowering my Black male students. This was urgent for me, and I had to protect my urgency if my vision was going to become my reality.

So I ask you, where does your urgency lie and how do you protect it? It is one thing to have a sense of urgency, but it is something entirely different to be able to sustain it. In the case of Black male students, it was not an overnight fix. Toward the end of protecting your sense of urgency, you have to understand that many endeavors may take time and you must remain committed to the goal, regardless of how long it may take to reach it. You cannot and must not allow setbacks, shortcomings, challenges, obstacles, failures, or disappointments to deter you from your sense of urgency because whatever it is that you deem to be urgent, I'm certain that it is in fact extremely so. Therefore, you must maintain your focus on protecting your sense of urgency toward seeing your goal to fruition. What's key is your level of commitment to the overall goal.

Q7 How am I protecting my leadership beliefs?

As a teacher, I taught in a school district that had an African American student population of well over 95 percent. I was more than convinced that a generic approach to educating African American children was not going to yield the results that the district, or I, desired. For a decade, I had studied and researched best practices for teaching African American students. As a result, I developed a set of beliefs that served as the foundation on which I stood for the 21 years that I served in schools. At the core of my beliefs was pedagogy that was culturally relevant. I was and continue to be unwavering in the notion that the youngsters I served had to be able to see themselves in the lessons and pages of the books. That is, they needed learning that was relevant, relatable, and identifiable. It was by approaching pedagogy this way that I was named school, district, and county Teacher of the Year after my fifth year of teaching. The answer to the question asked by many as to how I was so soon honored prestigiously at so many levels was simple: my students were achieving at high levels because what they were learning was culturally relevant. I taught in accordance with my beliefs, which were rooted in years of study.

My challenge as it related to my core belief was that I have always had colleagues who didn't share in my belief. I had colleagues and superiors who attempted to steer me away from it. But my belief was the foundation upon which I stood. My belief was everything I stood for as a teacher. Therefore, I had to protect my belief. I had to safeguard it, shield it, keep it from harm by standing firmly on what I believed and on what I knew with every fiber of my being predicated on our results. Had I not protected it, I may have felt compelled to transition to practices and strategies that would likely have yielded less desirable results. That is, I may have conformed or acquiesced, allowing my beliefs to be compromised. I believed strongly in what my students needed. I was staunch in my belief, and the results spoke for themselves. As a principal, I brought this same belief into my leadership (which I will discuss in the next question).

What about *you*?

As it relates to your leadership, what are your core beliefs? What unwavering beliefs do you hold? What beliefs do you hold that others might disagree with? What beliefs do you hold that others may have attempted to move you away from? What beliefs serve as the foundation for the work that you do? Have you experienced success through the implementation of your beliefs? Your beliefs got you into administration. Are you at a point in your career where you have taken complete ownership of your beliefs? If so, how are you protecting your beliefs?

Beliefs develop over time. My beliefs about culturally relevant pedagogy developed over a long period of time, and as they developed, I took ownership of them and claimed and embraced them. What about your leadership is unyielding and unwavering? For me it was culturally relevant pedagogy, which I took from the classroom to school leadership. What's key is how you go about protecting your beliefs and avoid having them compromised.

> *Protection Pointer:* Before you embrace a belief toward protecting it, the belief must be one that yields desired results. If the belief is strong but yields unfavorable results, protecting it will be difficult because there's no evidence that your belief is rooted in best practices. On the other hand, when there is solid evidence that your belief yields favorable results, protecting it becomes a no-brainer.

Say, for example, that your belief is that the oversight of teacher lesson planning is an effective bridge to developing meaningful and relevant collegial relations with teachers in a coaching capacity. If your administrative colleagues don't see the significance of administrative oversight of lesson plans and view it as a misuse of time, an additional responsibility, or an intrusion, they may attempt to dissuade you from expending the additional time and energy necessary to review lesson plans. For you, the oversight of lesson planning is a belief to which you hold firm, and you protect it by reminding yourself that your belief yields the intended results—a bridge to solid collegial relationships with the teachers that you supervise in a coaching capacity.

Q8 How am I protecting my leadership truth?

Of the 35 questions in this book, this is the one about which I am probably most passionate. This question builds on your beliefs and talks about your essence—who you are. As a leader, I had several truths that distinguished me from the pack, and I will discuss one here.

Beginning with my days as a classroom teacher, I never, ever began formal instruction before delivering a short morning message and engaging my students in a brief discussion about anything and everything, which I did every day of my career as a teacher. When I became an assistant principal, my principal delivered the morning message after the student-led morning announcements. On those days when the principal was out, I eagerly grabbed the microphone and spoke life into my school.

In my 14 years as a principal, a day never went by without delivering my morning message first thing. Having an athletic background, I am keenly aware that on game day, before the teams head onto the field, court, diamond, or ice, the head coach has something to say before the players leave the locker room. I took that practice with me to the classroom and to my principalship; it was my truth for starting the day, and I was going to protect it at all costs. I understood clearly the power and relevance of my morning message, particularly for my students who lost hope or simply had none. I strove to connect with these children daily through my morning message.

The true test of my truth was when a new superintendent appointed to my district scheduled our twice-monthly meetings for 8:00 a.m.—which would mean that, twice monthly, I would be unable to deliver my morning message. My morning message was my truth. I could not miss those two days. So I honed my people skills and explained to the superintendent why the message was important to the success of the school. He understood and scheduled the meetings for 9:00 a.m. I protected my morning message truth from being compromised.

What about *you*?

Do you have a truth? If so, what is it? Do you walk in your truth? Are you passionate about your truth? Does your truth drive your practice as a leader? Does your capacity as an assistant principal place limitations on your truth? Can you envision your truth enabling you to one day have an impact as a principal? Is your truth consistent with the existing culture of your school? Is your truth consistent with the various changes that may be needed in your school? Does your truth support the mission and vision of your school? Is your truth undeniably your own?

These are important questions to consider and to ask yourself in your assistant principal capacity relative to your truth generally. Interestingly, given the difference between the assistant principalship and the principalship, the manifestation of one's truth could be drastically different in the two roles. For example, my truth was the significance of the morning message. The problem was that in my time as an AP, the principal wanted to deliver the message, and rightfully so. Although the concept of a daily morning message was my truth, it was only manifested in the rare instances that the principal was absent. When I became principal, I walked in my truth daily.

As you are projecting to one day being principal, you must consider your truths—your core values, nonnegotiables, nondebatables as a leader—simultaneously. They are who you are as a leader and as a human being. I attempted to work in an environment where my truth was forced to take a back seat, and I went along with it. What enabled me to protect this particular truth during my tenure as an assistant principal was my vision of a principalship, which I felt was on the horizon. My vision was the protection that my truth required.

How are you going to be an effective leader if your truth, and you, have taken a back seat? That is, how are you going to be an effective leader if you allow your very essence to be compromised? As desperately as so many of us desire these administrative positions, you cannot be optimally effective if you have suppressed your essence in order to secure such a position. Just as you are being interviewed, you must also interview the interviewer to determine if the position is the best fit for you and your truth. You must protect your truth at all costs because when you protect your truth, you protect yourself.

Q9 How am I protecting my leadership spirit?

One of the things that I know about myself as a leader is that my spirit has to be stable and balanced. When I say my spirit, I mean my psyche, my inner being, my temperament, my energy. I will be the first to admit that through my 14 years of AP and principal leadership, there were times when my spirit felt completely broken, compromised, violated, or unbalanced. These were the toughest days to lead because I simply wasn't myself. I wasn't at ease.

> *Looking Back.* For a long time I worked with one of my troubled young men to help him get on the right path so that he could live out his potential. My reputation for successfully working with such young men was solid in the community. One day, a mother took issue with my sometimes stern approach with her son and let me have it—in front of her son (whose father was not in his life and who'd been infatuated with the streets and the gang life since he was in 6th grade). I was determined to save this young man from himself and the streets. His mother did not understand my long-term relationship with her son and what we were building. Her verbal attack undermined everything I was building with her son. I was never able to get our relationship back to where it needed to be, and he eventually succumbed to the streets.

It took me a few days to recover from that incident. My spirit had been broken because I was so invested in my young men—the reason that I got into education in the first place. In that instance, I hadn't protected my spirit. It was not safeguarded and was vulnerable. As time passed and I found myself in challenging situations that could possibly compromise my spirit, I recalled how I handled the aforementioned situation and was prepared for them emotionally. I was now prepared to protect my spirit by not owning the situation at hand and remaining conscious of my worth and value to the school and community.

What about *you*?

How do you go about protecting your leadership spirit? Does your spirit influence your leadership? Does your leadership influence your spirit? Are you able to separate yourself emotionally from situations where your character, values, beliefs, or truth are called into question? If your spirit is compromised, how do you get it back to where you need it to be?

There will certainly be times when, out of nowhere, things happen that affect you emotionally/spiritually. Myriad things can occur within a school community that can break a person down. A spirit buster for me was when one of my hardest-working, high-achieving students got jumped by four or five students from another school on the way home because he "looked smart." It took me a couple of days to recover from the sight of my student laying in a hospital bed with a black eye and broken jaw. As difficult as that was, I had a school to lead and students and staff who needed me to be myself. Again, I learned that I needed to protect my spirit because of the significance of my role as leader. I had to protect my spirit by compartmentalizing my pain and sadness for my student and not allowing this situation to adversely affect the spirit that I needed to bring to the rest of my students and staff.

It needs to work the same way for you. When challenging and difficult situations arise, you must steadfastly remind yourself that there's a school that needs you to be at your best. You must have the internal mechanisms to empathize while keeping your spirit focused on the work that lies ahead. You must be able to protect your spirit from being compromised.

Q10 How am I protecting my leadership happiness/joy?

If I don't know anything else, I know that you cannot be your best you over a prolonged period of time if you are not happy in the work you do. If you are going to perform optimally, it's got to be a joy to get up in the morning and prepare for the challenges that lie ahead.

In 2004, in my capacity as a middle school principal, my happiness and joy for the work I loved was completely compromised. The direction of the district had shifted dramatically and the impact that it had on my school was regrettable. Coming to school every day was a burden for me emotionally, and while I was in the school, I was simply going through the motions toward keeping the school afloat. I brought not an ounce of happiness, joy, or passion to my leadership that school year. I was preoccupied with the question, "What will I do next?" I had hit rock bottom in my leadership. (Just writing about it here is emotional for me.) I did not and could not protect my happiness in that situation. I was at a point of no return. The damage was irreparable.

Another school district was aware of my skill set and recruited me for the following school year to lead their lowest-performing high school. I gladly accepted their offer. I fell in love with the school from the first day and was there for six years before moving on to do the work that I do now. I was on fire every single day, even those days when my happiness could have justifiably been compromised. I'd learned how to protect my happiness— to keep situations or people from undermining it. I understood that in my previous district I was at the point of no return. I was in a district that was no longer compatible with my essence.

> *Protection Pointer:* We sometimes in life have to accept that not all situations are a good fit for us. Or that what was once a good fit deteriorated or turned into something dramatically different than it was. We have to know when to walk away to find true happiness. That is, we must find the courage to walk away.

In my new school, I found true happiness. I found a school that felt like it was built for me. My newfound happiness enabled me to operate at a very high level. In my fifth year there, I drew the attention of the Milken Family Foundation, which on December 1, 2009, bestowed me with the Milken Educator Award—the greatest achievement of my professional career. In my six years at that school, I never allowed my happiness to be compromised.

What about *you*?

Does your present role give you a sense of fulfillment? Do you feel that you are making a difference in the lives of the students and staff that you lead? Do you feel appreciated and respected? Do you feel that you belong in the school where you work? Is it a joy to walk into your building every day? Are you happy in your present role? Let me add my voice to the chorus of voices who have said to you or will say to you that every day isn't going to be a great day, every season isn't going to be a great season, every year isn't going to be a great year, and every appointment isn't going to be a great fit. There will be days, seasons, years, or appointments that are so adversely overwhelming that you question your decision to enter the ranks of school leadership. To compound my contention, you may be one who's going to challenge a status quo that you deem counterproductive to the students you serve—which may unsettle a number of people in a variety of capacities. As well, it could lead to isolation and working in an environment that becomes so hostile that sustaining joy and happiness is virtually impossible. My question to you in this regard is, how will you protect your happiness in that situation?

Everyone's professional situation, aspirational situation, purpose, mission, vision, agenda, sense of job security, and financial situation is different; to find and protect your happiness within your leadership, you've got to weigh each of these. It's not about you comparing yourself to others. Your situation is your own. You've got to weigh your situation against your reality and determine how you will be able to make your reality work for you. And within making your reality work for you, you've got to determine what measures will keep you happy. As you discover what makes you happy within your leadership, you must deliberately guard, shield, and protect it because, again, you cannot be your best you over a prolonged period of time if you are not happy in the work you do. If you are going to perform optimally, it's got to be a joy to get up in the morning and prepare for the challenges that lie ahead.

Protecting My Leadership Fervor

This chapter will focus on your leadership fervor and how to protect it.

What I mean by *fervor* is the level of intensity that you bring to your leadership as an assistant principal. When I am talking to an assistant principal or principal, it is not uncommon for me to ask, "How badly do you want to become great at what you do? How badly do you want to see your students attain success? How badly do you want to see your teachers grow professionally? How badly do you want your school to soar?" These questions refer to the leader's fervor, which must be protected.

I would venture to say that you cannot reach optimal success as an assistant principal if you don't approach your leadership with fervor—the level of intensity and passion that you bring to your leadership daily.

Let's now break down protecting the assistant principal leadership fervor.

Q11 How am I protecting my leadership *convictions*?

This is a big one—your convictions. I've had to protect convictions of mine that were not necessarily shared by others. For example, the biggest buzz word in education (as of this writing) is by far *equity*, which is not a new concept. The only thing new about it is that a previously unnamed practice has been embraced by more educators than previously. Equity has been a conviction of mine throughout my 35 years in education. But something peculiar happened in education following the murder of George Floyd on May 25, 2020, that caused the country to shift. Per the title of one of my blog posts, equity is not a four-letter word, the boogeyman, a political statement, or the enemy; *it's just great teaching*! I define equity as meeting young people where they are, as they are. That's it. I consider that simply great teaching, and it is one of my core and unwavering convictions in education. Where I have been challenged as a consultant is in the post–George Floyd space in which we find ourselves. More than a few clients have requested that I refrain from using the word equity in my presentations. Yes, you read that right. *I have been asked to refrain from using the word.* I have essentially been asked not to discuss either meeting young people where they are as they are *or* great teaching as it relates to the individual needs of learners in a classroom. I don't know how, nor do I possess the ability, to refrain from talking about equity when I am speaking to an audience of educators in light of my definition of the word. The whole idea goes hand in glove with great teaching. I protect my convictions and deliver my message in a way that just makes sense, so without using the word equity, I discuss equitable classroom practices in depth, ensuring that everyone in the room hears me loud and clear. If I feel that wouldn't be possible, I simply decline the invitation to present. Doing otherwise would result in me compromising and violating my conviction that what every youngster who enters a classroom requires at their core is a teacher who is committed to meeting them where they are, as they are.

What about *you*?

You are knowledgeable in a plethora of areas in education in general and leadership in particular. Within your areas of expertise, where do your convictions lie? In what areas can no one sway your thinking? In what areas would conflict result due to your deep convictions if, for example, your direct supervisor approached them differently? How would you handle it if your district launched a new initiative that was counter to your convictions? Would you conform for the greater good knowing that it runs counter to everything that you stand for, believe, and hold dear? How would you protect your conviction?

> *Protection Pointer:* Tough situations may arise and you'll have some tough choices to make, because we are not simply talking about your beliefs and opinions here; we are talking about your convictions, which are rooted in your leadership fervor. Communication is key. Relationships are key. Your people skills are key. Earned respect for your intellect is key. And ultimately, your protection of your convictions is key. When your convictions are incompatible with the requirements and expectations of your leadership, it's probably going to render you less than enthusiastic about your work as a leader. So you will need to carefully consider how you go about protecting your convictions.

As an assistant principal, protecting my convictions boiled down to reminding myself that I was not the leader of this school but would be in the near future. I was the assistant to the principal, and my role was to assist and support the vision of the principal while providing input where warranted and welcomed, which was dictated by the relationship that I had with the principal. I continually reminded myself that my day as the leader of a school would come. That was my protection.

Q12 How am I protecting my leadership optimism?

I can clearly recall my first day as an assistant principal. I had no idea what to expect. It was a middle school in New Jersey, and the school I had just left as a 5th grade teacher was one of its feeder schools and situated around the corner, which meant that I'd taught several students in the school. This put me at somewhat of an advantage because my former students put the "word on the street" that I was the "real deal." I also knew some of the teachers in the building (including one that I had grown up with), so my confidence in my new surroundings and my new role was rather high. I was quite optimistic that my first year was going to be a great one.

As I stated earlier, I was quickly relegated to the role of a disciplinarian, which included lunch duty and bus duty. I was also in charge of supplies, which entailed ordering supplies for teachers monthly via requisitions, maintaining the supplies/ monitoring the supply inventory, and delivering teachers' supplies to the classrooms—during instructional time. Yes, during instructional time!

Saying that I reached a point where I despised going to work would be an understatement. I knew that I was not going to grow under those circumstances. But the good thing is that my optimism for my future as a school leader was unaffected. I protected my optimism with every fiber of my being. I knew my worth, I knew my value, and I knew my potential. In my mind, the ceiling was high. I never lost sight of the fact that this bad situation was not my destiny; it was just a short stop on my road to principal leadership. My optimism for the future of my leadership was secure. My leadership fervor was intact. I just had to get through this rough patch while preventing my optimism from being compromised.

What about *you*?

In your current role or situation, are you optimistic about your professional growth and development? Are you optimistic about the possibility for advancement to a principalship? Are you optimistic that your assistant principalship is a stop on the way to the principalship? Are you optimistic that your talents and skill set are known by the decision makers in your district? Are you optimistic that your school is on the right path because of your leadership? Are you optimistic that a school will one day be in a good place because you are its principal? Are you optimistic that a future assistant principal will be the recipient of great leadership coaching from you when you are a principal?

I could go on and on. I am encouraging you to look deeply at your optimism as an assistant principal and a possible future principal. Your optimism about your leadership matters. If you are going to perform at a high level, there are many variables that matter—and one of those core variables is your optimism.

> *Protection Pointer:* Regardless of how difficult, challenging, seemingly unfair, or overwhelming the work may be, your optimism cannot and must not be adversely affected or compromised. Your belief in yourself and your confidence in yourself must remain high.

You got to the assistant principalship because of your previous accomplishments. You are talented. You must never lose sight of this, which translates to you intentionally protecting your optimism.

Q13 How am I protecting my leadership persistence?

As a principal of four schools over 14 years, all I knew were schools that were low-performing upon my arrival. The schools were located in economically disadvantaged neighborhoods where the residents were families of color. This is the only demographic that I know as an educator. Let me say emphatically that I loved working in that environment and wouldn't have had it any other way. However, it was not easy work. Although it was also rewarding work, it was replete with challenges that my suburban counterparts seldom, if ever, experienced.

Because the state assessment scores at one school were extremely low one year, I decided that we needed an additional morning of instruction. So I instituted a Saturday Morning Academy, which comprised four hours of instruction for my tested grade levels. Although I believed in my students and staff wholeheartedly, I knew that the students, who resided in historically marginalized communities, needed more. As optimistic as I was about the prospects for that year, I knew that the Saturday Morning Academy would take them over the top.

The problem, as I soon discovered, was that I could only get a handful of the students to come out on Saturdays. So that meant that I had to go harder to ensure that my vision and effort were aligned. My team and I worked hard to get parent buy-in. We also provided breakfast. As our efforts increased, my vision of Saturday attendance that matched our weekday attendance began to become a reality. I had to protect my persistence. I could not allow the initial low attendance to discourage me into conceding that our students would not attend school on a Saturday morning. I refused to quit on my students. I stepped up my game and, as a result, our assessment scores were not only the highest in the district at the middle school level—they were the highest of schools of similar demographics across the state of New Jersey!

What about *you*?

There are going to be countless times when your beliefs, convictions, confidence, optimism, passion, purpose, mission, vision, and goals are going to be put to the test. And you may at times question your convictions. Assistant principal and principal leadership is not easy work. The challenges and the volume of decisions you will make are ongoing. You must be able to think on your feet every day all year long. Once your persistence is compromised, your forward movement has been compromised. As a leader of a school, whether as an assistant principal or a principal, you can't effectively lead if your forward movement has been curtailed or you are moving in the opposite direction.

How are you protecting your persistence? How are you preventing the challenges that accompany leadership from compromising your persistence? How are you keeping your motivation high to continue to move forward even during difficult times? How are you maintaining your persistence when the decisions you make aren't necessarily embraced by all? How are you maintaining your persistence when your leadership reality goes through a rough patch? Toward maintaining your persistence, you must protect it. Your protection of your persistence is your ongoing reminder to yourself of your purpose, mission, and vision for leading, which includes your ongoing self-reflection and self-assessment of your leadership.

Q14 How am I protecting my leadership *perseverance?*

Closely related to your leadership persistence is your leadership perseverance. You've got to be able to persevere. You've got to be able to protect your leadership perseverance during difficult and challenging times.

Admittedly, I was an outspoken leader on issues about which I am passionate. As a leader, I was extremely outspoken on behalf of my students. I was an unapologetic advocate for my students' academic, social, and emotional well-being. I could not and would not allow my students to be shortchanged, overlooked, neglected, taken advantage of, marginalized, or ignored. Being outspoken is not for everyone, though, and without knowing you or your circumstances, I certainly won't recklessly suggest that you be that sort of leader. When you are outspoken, you'd better have a backup plan. (I always had a Plan B, Plan C, Plan D, and Plan E, which gave me leverage.) The thing is that when you are outspoken on behalf of your students, you're inevitably going to create some challenges and obstacles for yourself. It comes with the territory—it's the politics of education. And boy did I create some challenges and obstacles for myself. For three years, leadership life got very interesting and challenging and was downright overwhelming. But through it all, I protected my leadership perseverance, plowing right through it all because I was determined to win. My philosophy has always been if I win, my students win. Conversely, if I lose, my students lose. I refused to lose because I wasn't in education for my students to lose. Therefore, I had to persevere through that most challenging time of my leadership tenure. How? I kept my *why* close to the vest while daily reminding myself of my reason for entering the ranks of school leadership, never losing sight of the great leaders of the past that I admired and who also faced and endured great challenges because they dared to go against the grain. Two personal examples for me would be Jackie Robinson and Bill Russell. Both, as is widely known, endured extreme obstacles—and extreme racial hatred—and persevered. I studied them. I wanted to know what kept them motivated and able to persevere. The lessons that I learned from these leaders taught me how to protect my leadership perseverance; had I not, my leadership tenure would have ended prematurely.

What about *you*?

As an assistant principal, if you haven't discovered it yet, there will be times when it feels like someone has placed a brick wall in your path. Moreover, there will be times when that brick wall feels like four walls surrounding you and you have been boxed in. That is not the time to quit, however. It's an inherent part of leadership. You chose leadership, and leadership is not a role where everything fits neatly into place like a puzzle. Leadership can be very messy, and you can go days or weeks not knowing what to anticipate from day to day. In leadership, you are leading both adults and children who have their own individual personalities and influences. As a leader, you don't know which way the wind is going to blow on any given day. You can only anticipate the future based on your experience with the school you lead and prepare accordingly, which guarantees nothing. Through all of the forthcoming uncertainties, you must persevere. You must protect your leadership perseverance by continuing to strategically push forward as the leader or one of the leaders in your school. Giving up can never be a solution. You must always be cognizant of the fact that challenges, obstacles, pressures, and demands are simply a part of leadership. Your challenge is how you endure, how you persevere. And you persevere by protecting your leadership perseverance through understanding that the challenges are simply a part of the work that you signed up for.

In previous challenging situations, how did you persevere and protect your leadership perseverance? Have you ever allowed your perseverance to be compromised? If not, how did you prevent it? If so, how did you get yourself back on track? As a leader, how you protect your leadership perseverance matters because you cannot lead optimally if you lack the skill or ability to brave the storms you will inevitably encounter as a school leader.

Q15 How am I protecting my leadership excitement?

After my third year as a principal, I decided I wanted a change of scenery and left the city that raised me personally and professionally. I accepted a principalship in a city that I was very unfamiliar with and a district that quite frankly wasn't ready for me. (What I mean is that the district would have been more than ready for me after the 2020 murder of George Floyd. However, 20 years ago, it just wasn't a good fit for someone who brought a culturally relevant pedagogy/social justice education focus and perspective, which had been embraced in my previous district, to leadership.) While working in my new environment with the restrictions that were placed on who I was philosophically, I completely lost my excitement for leadership. It became a job that I did not want to wake up and go to. It was a low point in my professional life. To regain my excitement, I went into my people skills bag, and I gained some semblance of satisfaction. But as Dorothy in *The Wizard of Oz* said, "There's no place like home."

I tried as hard as I could to restore my excitement for my leadership in my new district, but I just couldn't be *me* in that environment. The excitement was gone. The fire had been extinguished. My excitement hadn't been protected. I thought that if I could return home where I could be me again, my excitement would return. Well, I *was* able to return to my original district, and the local newspaper even did a story on my return to welcome me back. I regained my excitement in that moment. From that point forward, I protected my excitement by being very particular about the environments in which I worked.

What about *you*?

Are you excited about being an assistant principal? Are you excited about the work that you do? Are you excited about your role as an assistant principal as outlined by your principal? Are you excited about your progress? Are you excited about your professional growth and development? Are you excited about the prospects for your future professionally? Are you excited about your students? Are you excited about the staff that you supervise? Are you excited about your school? Are you excited about the possibilities that each new day brings?

These are important questions to consider on a daily basis. It is one thing to walk in the work that you worked so hard to do. But it is something very different to walk in your work with excitement, which brings a whole different level of energy to the work. I would dare say that when you were in pursuit of your assistant principalship, the excitement that accompanied your pursuit was more than likely predictable. Once you got the position, however, not every aspect of it was as exciting as you may have anticipated. Some of it is just downright . . . work. But the aspects of your leadership that you consider exciting are those that you must savor, cultivate, and hold on to firmly. Those are the aspects of your leadership that you must protect while not letting anything nor anyone compromise or violate them.

> *Protection Pointer:* You must intentionally protect your excitement for those aspects of your leadership that regularly excite you while building excitement for the areas that do not.

Q16 How am I protecting my leadership obligation?

Because I know that the readership of this book will in all likelihood be racially diverse, I feel compelled to set up my thoughts here before I move forward. I am a Black man who was once a Black boy. As a Black boy, I dealt with certain challenges that were rooted in my being a Black boy, particularly while I was in high school. When I became a student of African American history—which has not adequately or truthfully been taught in America's classrooms—simultaneously, the world suddenly made sense to me, and I began to understand my challenges as a Black man in a historical context. In not knowing this history, I did not know a huge portion of myself. Because I did not know who I was historically, I had been living a life that was detached from its historical roots. I hadn't understood the collective dynamic of what it meant to be Black in America in general and a Black man in America in particular.

When I became a teacher and, later, a school administrator, I felt a certain obligation on so many levels to be extraordinary for my Black male students. I knew that they had similar, if not the same, challenges that I'd had growing up, including a lack of knowledge and understanding of who they were historically. I felt that I had an obligation to change that narrative. I made it my responsibility, both as a classroom teacher and a building leader, to ensure that my students in general and my male students in particular recognized fully who was looking back at them in their mirrors historically. For me, it was my leadership obligation. It wasn't something I'd learned in graduate school. This was personal. The challenge, though, was how I went about protecting my leadership obligation. What I set out to do was not always politically correct in an academic environment and, unless the staff and district officials were on the same page, could be considered controversial. As the protector of my obligation, I had to enlighten my young men and create opportunities to educate my staff and not fault them for what they'd never been exposed to.

What about *you*?

As a leader, you have infinite responsibilities. There will never be a day when you can sit back and say, "I have nothing to do." Those days simply don't exist. In leadership, there will always be something to do. Beyond your responsibilities are your passions, those aspects of your leadership that you are most enthusiastic about. But then there are also those aspects of your leadership about which you feel a certain obligation or you feel compelled. What I said about my obligation relative to Black male students could very easily fit into the category of responsibility or passion. But for me, it felt more like a calling—a duty, a moral imperative. It was my obligation.

What, if any, aspects of your leadership do you deem an obligation? Why do you consider them an obligation? Would any aspect of your leadership obligation be perceived as controversial by others? If so, how would you protect your sense of obligation, or would you abandon it? Would you allow it to be compromised although you deem it a moral imperative? These are important questions to consider as you reflect on your leadership obligation.

Q17 How am I protecting my leadership experience?

When I was a rookie assistant principal, my principal asked me to make 100 photocopies of the staff handbook that he compiled. The request was made on the last Friday of August in the afternoon, and the teachers were returning to school from summer break that following Tuesday, after Labor Day. The handbook was about 70 pages long. We had one large volume copier in the school, and it was not designed to collate 70 pages. This meant that I had to make 100 copies of each page separately and collate manually. Let that marinate for a moment. It took me all of Saturday, Sunday, and Monday because although the copier was high volume, it was not high speed. But by Tuesday morning, I handed the principal the boxes with the staff handbooks.

This happened 25 years ago, but it's still in me to this day. It stayed with me throughout my principalship—not because of the drudgery but because I never wanted to be guilty of treating anyone in my school in a similar fashion. I kept that experience close to the vest and ensured that I never asked anyone to do anything that I wouldn't do myself. I cannot fathom asking someone to spend a weekend on a project in the building while I am at home enjoying time with my family. I needed to protect that experience, which occurred very early in my leadership journey, as a reminder and an example of how not to treat the people who work for me, as opposed to simply dismissing it as a bad experience and moving on from it.

Most of you are going to move into a principalship. Along the way, you will accumulate a wealth of experience from your days as an assistant principal and as a teacher. Those years of experience are going to be invaluable to your continued leadership growth and development, particularly if you choose to move to the central office. You must protect those experiences. Throughout your leadership journey, you are going to encounter endless challenges, and how you handle them will be rooted in your collective leadership experiences. Those experiences will be your frame of reference. Although you will have grown in your leadership, you must never divorce or detach yourself from your experiences. They comprise who and what you are as a leader and are your foundation, and the lessons learned from them are immeasurable. You must protect your experiences by always leaning on them for guidance and not discount or run away from those that were less than favorable. I kept all of my experiences close to the vest; both the recent ones and the ones from the past that I would have preferred to have forgotten, such as the Labor Day weekend with the copier machine. We learn from our successes and failures and everything in between, so protecting those experiences matters.

What about *you*?

Making decisions doesn't necessarily happen in a vacuum. Our current decisions are often rooted in our previous experiences. That is, our previous experiences often influence current actions. In leadership, your previous experiences can never be ignored. How are you using your previous experiences to enhance your leadership? How are you using your previous experiences to inform your current decision making? How are you using your previous experiences to frame your current leadership practices? How are you using your previous experiences to enhance your leadership? How are you protecting your experiences as a leader? Again, when I say protecting your experiences, I mean intentionally making your experiences in leadership and beyond an integral part of your current leadership journey. Your previous experiences are who you are. You can never fully detach yourself from them because they are a part of your foundation. It is quite normal for me to share my most difficult years as an adolescent, a young man, a teacher, an assistant principal, a principal, and even as a presenter because they are the foundation on which I stand today. By not hiding or running away from them, I am essentially protecting them. You, too, must protect your experiences and use them as leverage to get where you want to go.

Q18 How am I protecting my leadership *work ethic?*

At the beginning of my career as a principal, I was an unapologetic workaholic. I put in 12 to 14 hours on weekdays and 16 hours on weekends . . . in the building. Looking back on it now, I put in that many hours because I simply didn't know better. My assistant principalship didn't prepare me for anything else. I boasted to people that I was putting in almost 90-hour weeks and challenged others to do the same. I measured my worth in part by the number of hours I lived in that school every week. Although I worked a tremendous number of hours, I didn't necessarily work smart for all of those hours. I was on the fast track to burnout, a mental or physical breakdown, and a lack of balance in my personal/family life. I had a solid work ethic but a substandard leadership work ethic. My work ethic as it was wasn't going to put me in a position to a long career—and longevity matters.

Over time, I learned how to recognize, acknowledge, and use the talents of the people around me and reduced my time in the building by 30 to 40 hours per week. This in turn brought balance to my life and made me more productive. I'd raised the level of my leadership work ethic and was no longer simply going through the motions of working. To sustain my newfound work ethic, I had to protect it by not allowing myself to slip back to where I was.

What about *you?*

In your assistant principal capacity, how many hours are you putting in each day and week? Are you putting in hours on the weekend as well? If so, how many hours? In what ways are you using the human capital around you? Have you contributed to the culture of your school in ways that make staff willing to do more? Is your work ethic productive for your school? How do you go about protecting your work ethic?

As was the case with me, there will be a temptation to put an exorbitant amount of time into your leadership, particularly when you are a new leader or preparing for a principalship. But putting in that much time does not necessarily translate to a good work ethic. It just means that you spend a lot of hours working, and many of those hours may be nonproductive or counterproductive. You must protect your work ethic by ensuring that your time spent on the job is productive. There are not enough minutes in the day to be counterproductive, particularly in leadership. Protect your work ethic by ensuring that you work hard . . . and smart.

Q19 How am I protecting my leadership attention to detail?

I don't think we can talk enough about attention to detail. Attention to detail is critical to your overall leadership. It's time-consuming, but it matters. As it relates to your day-to-day responsibilities, a macro approach to your work will translate to missing a ton of important smaller components of your leadership. Take instructional leadership, for example. When coaching a teacher in areas of deficiency, the details of the deficiency matter. Avoiding the details could undermine the objectives associated with coaching the teacher. In terms of discipline, an incident could arise between students that necessitates that you launch an investigation. Depending upon the scope of the incident, the outcome of the investigation could have long-lasting implications. Therefore, the details can never be glossed over; they must be taken seriously and taken into account. Your attention to detail must be protected. Allowing it to be compromised could prove disastrous in a given situation.

> *Looking Back:* When I became a school administrator, several students that I taught became my students again in my capacity as a middle school assistant principal. My new school was three middle schools housed in one building—separate entities with common areas used by all three schools. In the basement was a thruway used to travel to the common areas such as the gym, cafeteria, auditorium, library, and swimming pool. One day there was an incident involving boys from all three schools. Regarding the students involved from my school, I investigated the situation thoroughly and imposed suspensions. Ten years later, one of the suspended students, then an adult, stopped by the school I was leading at that time to see me. During our conversation, he brought up the incident of 10 years earlier. He said, "Mr. Kafele, you are a great principal, but you got that one wrong. I told you then, and I'm telling you now, I had no involvement in that incident." I missed a detail, and I will be haunted by that mishap forever.

What about *you*?

In your role of assistant principal, you are in a role of non-stop decision making. You have to be able to make quick decisions, but they have to be the right decisions. You must be able to think on your feet while always making decisions that are rational as opposed to emotional. Within your decision making, you must pay particular attention to detail. I missed a small detail that caused a young man to miss three days of school and, I'm sure, suffer a degree of punishment at home.

Attention to detail goes far beyond discipline, though. Every aspect of your leadership requires detail, and some situations require more than others. I am one to say that in terms of the purpose of children attending our schools every day, the number one reason is to learn. If they are going to learn optimally, they must be in a learning environment that is conducive to optimal learning where they report to an excellent teacher every day. Your collegial relationship with this teacher is crucial. Not every youngster has the opportunity to walk into a classroom with an excellent teacher. Your attention to detail relative to the professional growth of a teacher will matter exponentially. You must plan to spend sufficient time examining the nuances of a teacher's pedagogy toward helping her become the excellent teacher that your students require. That is, your planning, organization, and time management must be such that you are able to effectively protect your attention to detail. Otherwise, you will not be in a position to assist a teacher with pedagogical development.

Reflecting on your own attention to detail, how would you assess yourself? Are you one who pays attention to detail? Are you able to examine detail while simultaneously being able to manage your overall time so that you are not overwhelmed or inundated by the particulars of a situation? Are you able to maintain your composure while working through a potentially detailed and tedious situation? Are you proficient in planning, organization, and time management? Attention to detail is not necessarily easy, but it is an essential component to your overall effectiveness as a school leader.

Q20 How am I protecting my leadership resilience?

As a presenter, I am asked often to speak on the topic of diversity, equity, and inclusion (DEI). I have been quite conversant in this area since 1988. Interestingly, though, the invitations to present on this topic were few and far between until after the murder of George Floyd. The country shifted after George Floyd's murder, and countless schools and organizations began to realize that they actually needed training in DEI.

Prior to George Floyd's murder, it was glaring for me that although there were districts that invited me in to present on DEI, many in the audiences were not ready for the uncomfortable conversation. (I customarily ask the principal or superintendent who invites me if the school or district is ready for the uncomfortable conversation. The typical response is something like, "Whether or not we are ready, we need it." I take that as a no.) The tension in the room around the topic is typically quite palpable. However, no one ever said anything or behaved in a way that was disrespectful until 2018, when I spoke to a district in my home state of New Jersey. The district had a large Black student population and a large white teacher population. I was invited to present because teacher–student relations were not healthy. For the first time in my life, I was loudly, repeatedly, and disrespectfully heckled by a teacher, as if I were a standup comedian. When, after some time, the administration intervened, the teacher was given a "time out" and allowed to return to the auditorium about 20 minutes later. Wow! Moments after the teacher's return, the entire high school staff abruptly stood up and noisily walked out of the auditorium—while I was speaking—while the elementary and middle school staffs remained. Again, wow! (One teacher, a very young white woman, walked onto the stage and looked me in the eyes and said I was an insult to the entire district.) Through all of that, I presented for another couple of hours to the staff that remained. The topic of DEI can be quite uncomfortable indeed.

I can go into much more detail about that day, but I will leave it there. Being fully transparent, that experience broke me. Yes, I was a broken presenter that day. I returned to my car in the parking lot at 4:00 p.m. and cried and cried and cried. I cried not because of what happened to me but because I knew that those same educators would return to classrooms to teach children the next morning. I was invited in because of the teachers' classroom practices and poor relationships with their students. I had witnessed firsthand what the administration had complained about. It was three hours before I could start my car and drive home. I sat there and cried on and off while calling my wife and mother to share with them what I'd experienced. I sat there broken. My resilience was compromised and unprotected. I momentarily lost my focus and my *why* and was oblivious to the fact that this is precisely why I do this work. When I got home, I was still broken and cried once again. Later that evening, a handful of the teachers took to social media and posted racial epithets aimed at me. It was an unreal, unforgettable experience. It wasn't until I woke up the next morning that I challenged myself. I had to get ahold of myself. I asked myself, "What are you doing, and why are you allowing these people to break you?" My internal conversation went along those lines. I quickly recalled my why and regained my focus. I had to remind myself that my experience was the reason I was invited into that district in the first place. I bounced back and was ready for my next audience. I have never since allowed challenging situations to break me. I am very cognizant of the need to always protect my resilience, the intentionality of bouncing back after setbacks.

What about *you*?

You are going to have setbacks. I repeat, you are going to have setbacks. Setbacks are inevitable with anything in life, including the assistant principalship. What's key is your ability to bounce back. Let's look at a scenario. You spend the entire year coaching a teacher who is struggling relative to student achievement. You give your all to this teacher practically weekly with the necessary attention to detail. You are pleased with the teacher's ongoing progress relative to the overall performance pedagogically in the classroom. You do not feel that any stones were unturned. His students take the state standardized assessments in the spring, and the aggregate scores decreased to levels that were significantly lower than when you began coaching him. You feel defeated. You feel deflated. You repeatedly ask yourself what went wrong. In that moment, you don't feel that there's anything you could have done better or differently, and you begin to question your own ability and skill set. For a period of weeks, your confidence is lost, and you are finding it difficult to bounce back. In this moment, your resilience has been compromised.

Have you ever found yourself in a similar situation? Did you bounce back from it? How did you bounce back from it? What role did your principal play in helping you to bounce back? Was the principal supportive, or did the principal's reaction compound your deflation? How do you typically handle set-backs? Do you anticipate them and consequently prepare your-self for them emotionally with a plan to overcome them when they arise?

In the scenario detailed, I am going to expect excellence from the teacher but will always anticipate the worst and create a Plan B, Plan C, Plan D, and Plan E in the event that Plan A doesn't pan out. In this challenging role called the assistant principalship, you must prepare yourself for the unexpected and be intentional about not letting the work or aspects of it break you. You must be mindful of the fact that you are a human being and will make mistakes. Perfection will seldom, if ever, occur. So when you have that setback, if you need to wallow in it for a minute, go on and wallow in it . . . but only for a minute. Rather than letting one minute become two or three minutes, begin to formulate your plan to bounce back from whatever setbacks may have arisen, and stick to your plan.

Again, looking at the scenario, you would analyze the teacher's data and reflect on your interactions with the teacher over time, including reviewing all notes you may have taken. Look deeply at your coaching and the overall collegial relationship, includ-ing your classroom visits. I promise you will identify areas that you need to approach differently moving forward. This is how you go about protecting your leadership resilience while you prepare to bounce back.

CHAPTER 3

Protecting My Leadership Authenticity

n recent years, I have observed that the word "authenticity" has gained the attention of a lot of people in various walks of life. In the education leadership space, there's an ongoing debate relative to the extent to which one can be authentic in their capacity as a leader. People typically want to be themselves and not compromise who they are. As a leader, I desired to be and was my authentic self. However, there were costs associated with my intentional authenticity. Eventually, I was able to distinguish my authenticity outside school from my authenticity in school. As I say to many of my audiences, I learned to distinguish "Baruti Kafele" from "Principal Kafele." Of course, Baruti Kafele informed and influenced Principal Kafele, but I grew in a way that enabled me to keep them separate while keeping Principal Kafele true to himself.

To be clear, and I want you to hear me well on this, new—first day, first week, and perhaps first month or so—Assistant Principal Kafele had no authenticity. I hadn't been on the job long enough to know who I was going to become as a leader. My authenticity came with time. I had a lot to learn about myself as a leader and all aspects of the role of leader within a school and a complex organization, a school district. I don't believe that a new assistant principal or principal initially has an authenticity to protect. Your authenticity develops as you simultaneously figure out your leadership and your new role and who you are or are going to become as a leader. As you come into who you are going to become and are satisfied with how you've evolved, then the business of protecting your authenticity becomes a real thing.

This final and 15-question chapter is all about protecting your leadership authenticity, once your leadership becomes authentically you. The challenge of protecting your leadership authenticity differs from the challenges associated with protecting your leadership mindset and fervor. Protecting your leadership authenticity is essentially protecting your leadership essence, which I deem critical. When your essence is compromised, the person in your mirror can become unrecognizable.

Let's now break it down.

Q21 How am I protecting my leadership brand?

By "brand" I am referring to two things: your brand *identity* and your brand *image*. Brand identity tells you *about* a person and allows you to distinguish the person from countless others. Brand image refers to the way that a person's brand is being *perceived* or *interpreted*. The problem arises when the two are not aligned—that is, when you see yourself one way but are perceived in a very different way.

When I was a 5th grade teacher, I was the only Black man in my school, and Black women were in the minority. The majority of the teachers were white. One year for Black History Month, I wore African attire and took my students deeper into African and African American history and culture than I typically did. As all of my students were Black, I wanted them to be well versed in their history and culture. I wore African attire to fully represent what I was teaching. (Teaching Black history was a huge part of my overall brand identity as a teacher all year, not only in February. As my colleagues were aware, I intentionally crafted that brand.) When I wore my African attire during the month of February, I was simply reinforcing what my brand identity was all about. However, some of my white colleagues had difficulty with my authenticity/brand identity; it was obvious that they were uncomfortable with what I represented. Their perception of me, or the brand image of me that they'd created, ran counter to who I was and what I was about. I saw myself as teaching, encouraging, inspiring, and empowering my students to have pride in who they were historically and culturally. (To this day, the freedom to instill this historical and cultural pride in Black children in America's schools continues to be an uphill battle.) Those particular teachers took issue with me and perceived me to be a racist. They didn't understand that teaching Black history and essentially inculcating Black pride in the children is not teaching anti anyone. The beauty is that they confronted me about the image they created about my brand, and I was able to educate them. They truly hadn't understood. Had they not approached me, I would never have known how they perceived me, and who knows what the long-term implications of their perception and interpretation of me could have been. Because we had the conversations, I was able to reconcile my brand identity with how I was being perceived and the brand image that the teachers had of me. I was able to protect my brand identity from being distorted or maligned by individuals who simply didn't understand while maintaining my classroom authenticity.

What about *you*?

What do leadership brand identity and image mean to your leadership? What is your leadership brand identity? How do you wish to be perceived within your leadership capacity? Is how you wish to be perceived consistent with how you are being perceived? Have you been intentional about establishing your brand identity? Have you shaped your own brand identity, or did circumstances external to you shape it for you? Are your brand identity and your brand image compatible? Is your brand identity compatible with your school's purpose, mission, vision, and culture? What measures have you taken to protect the authenticity of your leadership brand identity?

These are important questions to consider in your assistant principal capacity and later in your capacity as a principal. As I always say, your staff aren't following you per se; they are following their perception of who you are. There's a big difference, and you must be aware of it. As an assistant principal, just by virtue of the fact that you hold that title, you have a brand identity. What's key is that you are the creator, molder, shaper, controller, and owner of your brand identity. You must be very intentional about how you are being seen and perceived. You must protect your brand identity, which speaks to your leadership authenticity. If you don't create, mold, shape, control, and own your own brand identity, your staff will do those things via the brand image that they have of you—and *that's* the person they will follow. You must intentionally, deliberately, and purposefully clarify who you are in both word and action. You must protect your leadership brand identity from being compromised.

Q22 How am I protecting my leadership competency and *credibility*?

I will never, ever forget my first day, week, or month as a new assistant principal. As soon as I walked into the building on January 2, 1998, several of the teachers had questions for which I didn't have answers. I'd been teaching 5th graders just 10 days earlier! When I walked into my new school as an administrator, it didn't matter to the teachers that I was new. They had issues and challenges that they needed resolved. They had concerns about behaviors of students that I did not know and field trips that I knew nothing about. They had concerns about issues carried over from December (when I was still in the classroom) and about teacher supply orders, which I learned that day would be one of my primary responsibilities. Through all of this, I embraced my new role and demonstrated competence. I didn't have all of the answers immediately, but I was able to respond to them all in a way that let them know that their concerns mattered. I asked lots of questions and followed up on everything asked of me. I am sure that in the teachers' eyes, I needed to come in as a strong and capable leader, and that was what I strove to do. Although I didn't yet possess the competence and credibility as a school leader, I came in qualified in an assistant principal capacity. What I initially and intentionally protected—my qualifications to lead—were the competency and the credibility that I possessed at that juncture of my leadership journey. Whenever I felt challenged or overwhelmed in those early days, my reminders to myself that I belonged were my credentials and qualifications. I refused to lose sight of either. They were my protection.

What about *you*?

There is an unwritten expectation that school leaders will be competent in multiple areas, including areas in which you may not yet be competent. As an assistant principal and a principal, it starts with who you are, your credentials, and your outlook. Your staff need to know who you are and what you are about. I compare this to when I speak. Everyone in that audience isn't going to know me. Many may never have heard of me. Therefore, I insist that my bio is read in its entirety so that I can establish some level of competency and credibility with my audience before I deliver my message. At a bare minimum, your staff should know the following about you:

» Your educational background,

» Your work experience, including your accomplishments,

» Your educational philosophy, including your education blog page and YouTube channel (if you have either),

» Your purpose for leading as an assistant principal, and

» Your vision for your leadership as an assistant principal.

These are absolutely essential to demonstrate your competence and establish credibility with staff. Your competence and credibility must be protected as you move forward.

Beyond the start of your assistant principal tenure, there are some questions that you've got to ask yourself regularly, such as, am I competent to speak intelligently on a given topic relative to the work that I do? Do I possess the expertise to competently coach the teachers I supervise on a variety of instructional methodologies? Am I perceived by my staff and students as a competent and credible leader? Do staff accept my advice and suggestions as credible? What about my background would make my staff consider me a competent and credible leader? What about my leadership would make my staff consider me a competent leader? Do the members of my leadership team consider me a competent and credible leader? How do parents perceive me as a leader? What measures have I taken to protect the authenticity of my leadership competency and credibility?

Protection Pointer: Over time as an assistant principal, you are going to develop a level of competency and credibility in the eyes of your staff and students. But what's key are the measures you take to protect them. Your competency and credibility must be protected by way of striving to continue to be the best version of yourself as a leader—always striving to grow as a leader and never resting on past successes. Your goal must always be to be better than you were and know more than you did the day before. That is how you go about protecting your leadership competency.

Q23 How am I protecting my leadership reputation?

As a new assistant principal and spending the bulk of my days addressing student behaviors, I grew increasingly frustrated. I could never get it out of my mind what I used to do every day— teach and inspire children in my classroom. I thought that I was going to bring that skill set to my assistant principalship and collaborate with teachers to take children to heights previously unimagined. My reality was very different. Although addressing student behaviors was frustrating, delivering supplies to the teachers during instructional time was *beyond* frustrating and humiliating. I felt that, as an assistant principal, the reputation that I had built as a teacher was on the line/at risk/taking a hit/being compromised. I increasingly began to dislike going to work every day. I did not feel like myself. I didn't feel whole in this new capacity because I knew that I was being underutilized. I had to do something, and quickly. I actually did a few things, one of which was the creation of what I called The Battle of the Homerooms, a schoolwide trivia competition in which questions were posed during the morning announcements. In Battle, each homeroom class was responsible for coming up with an answer, and one representative per homeroom would place the answer in a box in my office following the morning announcements. The culminating activity was a schoolwide assembly that I moderated. The six homeroom classes were represented by six students in the homeroom classes. The winning team received trophies, and the students in the winning homerooms were awarded a pizza party. That activity in part helped me to feel differently about my work and completely transformed the way I was perceived by students and staff. I created a space for myself where I was once again seen as an educator. My reputation in the eyes of students and staff had shifted—and the culture of the entire building shifted as well. I felt renewed. Key, though, was protecting my leadership reputation. This meant that I had to keep on creating new ways to make me feel like I mattered educationally to the school in a capacity other than disciplinarian while enhancing my reputation as a school leader.

What about *you*?

At the proverbial end of the day, all you have is your reputation. You must be very deliberate about protecting it at all costs. You've worked incredibly hard to build it. But the truth of the matter is that your reputation can be quite fragile and delicate—solid one moment and crash and burn the next. Every time you leave your home, your reputation is on the line. Every time you walk into your building, your reputation is on the line. Every time you walk out of your office, your reputation is on the line.

Every time you engage in a conversation, your reputation is on the line. Every time you take to social media, your reputation is on the line. It is very easy for your reputation to be compromised.

Your reputation as seen through the eyes of everyone who sees you matters, professionally *and* personally. You're not in a position to ignore how others feel about you. So ask yourself, what measures have I put in place to ensure that how I see myself is consistent with who I actually am? What measures have I put in place to ensure that how I see myself is consistent with how I am being perceived by staff, students, parents, and the community? How deliberate am I about safeguarding my reputation? If or when my reputation is compromised professionally or personally, would I be able to fight through it? What measures have I taken to protect the authenticity of my leadership reputation?

These are important questions to ask regarding your leadership authenticity to protect your leadership reputation. If you are going to lead at a high level over the long haul, how you protect your reputation as a leader can never be minimized. Once your reputation as a leader has been compromised, it will be difficult, if not impossible, to restore it. And remember, you are not solely an assistant principal when you are in your school. You are an assistant principal when you are away from school and on your own time. You do not know when you are going to run into current or former students. You could run into them *anywhere*, as I have. Imagine that you run into a student somewhere outside of school and your behavior is in stark contrast to that displayed to your students and staff. In that moment, your reputation has likely been compromised. Protecting your reputation must always be a priority.

Q24 How am I protecting my leadership people skills?

As an educational leader, your people skills absolutely matter. You are not going to achieve optimal results if your people skills are deficient. As an assistant principal, you are in the people business. As such, having strong skills in working with, interacting with, dealing with, and leading people is nonnegotiable. If you do not have strong people skills, it behooves you to develop them.

Often in seminars that I conduct, I challenge my audience to visit a local car dealership and have a brief conversation with the top salesperson. I tell them to get the person to tell them what makes them a top salesperson. I tell them that the person will not say they move so many cars because they know cars, the features of cars, or the benefits of cars. I tell them that there's a high probability that the salesperson will tell them that they move as many cars as they do because they know and understand people. In other words, they as quickly as possible forge a relationship with the individual who walks into the showroom. That requires a high degree of people skill because the meeting is not organic. The salesperson wants to eat, and selling cars is what allows them to do so. The person who enters the showroom may simply want to look around and have no intention of making a purchase. People skills turn a person who may have no interest in a new car into the owner of a new automobile. People skills matter.

What about *you*?

I have a lot to say about people skills. Your people skills can make or break your leadership. As an educator and, in this case, an assistant principal, you are in the people business, which requires that you have superior skills in dealing and engaging with people.

I will begin by focusing on your verbal and nonverbal communication skills when communicating with groups and interpersonally and end with your written communication skills. I am asking you to consider the underlying, self-reflective question, *are my verbal, nonverbal, and written communication skills an asset to my leadership?* My focus for your verbal and nonverbal communication skills will be your communication skills at your staff meetings. I could talk about the parent meeting, student meeting, community meeting, board meeting, and interpersonal communication, but there is a ton of overlap here.

Verbal communication (and the staff meeting). I want you to take a look at the following 18 self-reflective questions and ask yourself how they apply to who you are in a staff meeting:

> » How do I open my meetings to simultaneously capture the attention of my staff and engage them?
>
> » Am I able to capture the attention of my staff?
>
> » Am I able to command the room while establishing and sustaining an interest in the topic?
>
> » Are my staff attentive and engaged because of my leadership title or because of my leadership?
>
> » Am I skilled in the use of vocal variety (i.e., not monotone)?
>
> » Am I knowledgeable of and conversant in everything on the meeting agenda, and is it apparent in my delivery?
>
> » Am I confident in my leadership in this role?

» Am I able to put my staff at ease during challenging times?

» Am I able to own and sell district mandates I don't necessarily agree with?

» Have I developed the ability or the skill to make a meeting interesting?

» Am I respectful of my staff's time?

» Am I engaging (as opposed to being a lecturer)?

» How is my tone when I address my staff?

» How is my overall demeanor being perceived by staff (i.e., does my presence turn staff off)?

» Do I ever use staff meeting time as a personal gripe session?

» Do I ever use staff meeting time to complain about, criticize, or tear down one or more teachers without mentioning their names?

» Have I developed the skill to allow teachers to save face after they make comments I disagree with?

» Do I close my meetings in ways that get staff ready and motivated for the next day?

Each question is vitally important for you to consider in your assistant principal capacity. As you hold up your mirror, delve deeply into these questions and gauge whether there are adjustments that you need to make moving forward. As you make the adjustments to become an effective communicator at your staff meetings, remember that you must strive to protect the adjustments. The goal is to be an effective communicator. But if you fail to protect your gains by not being intentional about your effectiveness via asking yourself the aforementioned questions, you can easily lose them.

Nonverbal communication (and the staff meeting). As important as verbal communication is to your leadership, and in this case in a staff meeting, nonverbal communication is equally important. When you are in your leadership capacity, when you are not communicating verbally, you're communicating nonverbally. That said, I want you to take a look at the following seven self-reflective questions and ask yourself how they apply to who you are in a staff meeting:

» What message does my presence communicate?

» Does my presence communicate leadership?

» Does my posture communicate leadership?

» How do I use my space?

» What messages do my facial expressions convey?

» How do I make use of eye contact?

» Do my hand gestures enhance my nonverbal communication?

My point here is to remind you that just as your verbal communication skills are of paramount importance, so are your nonverbal communication skills.

Interpersonal communication. To round out this section on verbal and nonverbal communication, I want you to consider these 18 interpersonal characteristics with self-reflective questions that are absolutely vital to your credibility as a communicator:

» *Inspiring.* In my interpersonal communication with teachers, do they consider me an inspiring school leader?

» *Approachability.* In my interpersonal communication with teachers, do they consider me an approachable school leader?

» *Relatability.* In my interpersonal communication with teachers, do they consider me a relatable school leader?

» *Likability.* In my interpersonal communication with teachers, do they consider me a likable school leader?

» *Dependability.* In my interpersonal communication with teachers, do they consider me a dependable school leader?

» *Reliability.* In my interpersonal communication with teachers, do they consider me a reliable school leader?

» *Empathy.* In my interpersonal communication with teachers, do they consider me an empathetic school leader?

» *Compassion.* In my interpersonal communication with teachers, do they consider me a compassionate school leader?

» *Trustworthiness.* In my interpersonal communication with teachers, do they consider me a trustworthy school leader?

» *Listening skills.* In my interpersonal communication with teachers, do they consider me a good and sincere listener?

» *Ability to "read the room."* In my interpersonal communication with teachers, do they consider me a school leader who knows and understands them and their strengths and weaknesses and leads them accordingly?

» *Coaching skills.* In my interpersonal communication with teachers, do they consider me a solid coach who helps them develop pedagogically?

» *Cheerleading skills.* In my interpersonal communication with teachers, do they consider me a solid cheerleader who encourages them to develop pedagogically?

» *Equity.* In my interpersonal communication with teachers, do they consider me a school leader who demonstrates equity in my treatment of them and in my relationships with them?

» *Empowering.* In my interpersonal communication with teachers, do they consider me a school leader who strives to empower them to maximize their potential?

» *Collaboration.* In my interpersonal communication with teachers, do they consider me a collaborative school leader who strives to work with them toward maximizing their individual potential?

» *Problem-solving skills.* In my interpersonal communication with teachers, do they consider me a problem solver?

» *Servanthood.* In my interpersonal communication with teachers, do they consider my leadership to be about them and their roles as classroom teachers and not about me?

Written communication. I cannot overstate the significance of exemplary written communication skills. As an assistant principal, you will be expected to write in countless diverse situations. What you write will be read by a plethora of people. And trust and believe that attention will be paid to what you write beyond its intended meaning. Grammatical errors will not go unnoticed. You must ensure that your written communications are minimally compromised. Inadequate writing skills can severely undermine your credibility as a school leader. Your writing will be scrutinized by readers. A relevant question to ask of yourself then would be, how do I know if I am a proficient writer? My suggestion is to write a paragraph or an essay on any topic and share it, or something you've already written, with an accountability partner and gauge their response. Expect brutal honesty. If it turns out that your writing is deficient, you know you have work to do. Following are some of the forms of communication you will be required to write:

- » Staff bulletin/newsletter
- » Staff memo
- » Staff performance evaluations
- » Lesson plan feedback
- » Website statement
- » Incident reports
- » Reports to the principal
- » Reports to the superintendent
- » Reports to other stakeholders
- » Correspondence to central office administrators
- » Letters to parents
- » Correspondence to community stakeholders (e.g., invitations)
- » Emails to various stakeholders
- » Social media posts and blogs
- » Notes to staff and students

Of course, there are countless other scenarios where you will be expected to write, and as a leader at your school, the expectation is that you will be able to write proficiently.

To conclude, ask yourself, how do my current people skills compare with the aforementioned? How are my people skills being perceived by the people that I lead? How intentional am I about developing my people skills? How intentional am I about protecting my people skills? Are my people skills a priority in my overall leadership? Is there room for improvement?

I cannot overstate the significance of proficiency in your people skills in terms of your verbal communication, nonverbal communication, interpersonal communication, and written communication. Compromise in any of these areas can severely undermine your credibility as a leader and stifle your opportunities for advancement. You must protect them by striving to be proficient in each. If you need assistance, get it. Don't allow your pride or ego to stand in the way of you getting help to become proficient in these areas. You cannot be optimally effective if you're people-skill ineffective.

Q25 How am I protecting my leadership presence?

As a teacher, assistant principal, and principal, I was very cognizant of what I wanted my presence to represent. It was an aspect of my leadership that I didn't take lightly. It began with my appearance. As I delved deeply into reading and studying African and African American history upon entering undergraduate school, I developed a particularly strong interest in three historical figures: Martin Luther King Jr., Malcolm X, and Nelson Mandela. Although I read everything I could get my hands on regarding African and African American history, something about those three men completely captured my attention. I read and own over 40 books on their lives. I particularly zeroed in on their presence and what it represented to the masses of people worldwide who adored them. But the first thing that I noticed in photos of them was their appearance. They always had on a suit and tie. That inspired and influenced me. For my entire 21 years in public education, my students only saw me in a suit and tie. I wanted to appear as the ultimate professional for my students in general and my boys in particular. And believe me, they noticed. They would comment on my attire pretty much every day, and every now and then, one of my 5th grade boys would emulate me and wear a suit to school. I was ever so conscious of my presence, and I was clear from the feedback from my students that my presence mattered.

Beyond attire, however, was me—my essence. What did I represent as an educator? From day one, I thought about this deeply, and I concluded very early in my career that I wanted to represent excellence. I wanted to be about excellence. I wanted to set a standard of excellence in everything I did in the presence of my students and for my students, as both a teacher and an administrator. When the students saw me, I wanted them to see what I was intentionally representing: excellence. With that as my intention, I also had to be intentional about protecting it. Allowing my presence to be compromised could spell disaster for the credibility I earned from my students. It didn't mean I had to be perfect. Although I could make mistakes, my overall presence and demeanor had to be about representing the standard that I was setting for my students.

What about *you*?

What does your presence represent to your school? What does your mere presence in the building mean to your school's overall climate and culture? What message does your presence convey? What does your presence communicate without you ever opening your mouth? What does your presence represent to your students? What exactly do your students see when they observe you? When they listen to you, what exactly do they hear? When they think of you, what might come to mind? What does your presence represent to your staff? What does your presence represent to your principal and administrative colleagues? What does your presence represent to your students' parents? What does your presence represent to your school's community?

The aforementioned questions are vitally important questions for you to consider. Your presence as a leader and an assistant principal truly matters. Your presence is who you are when you are not speaking. Your presence speaks for you, and it speaks loudly. Your presence is your leadership representative; it enters the room before you do. The complicated part is that you cannot announce or proclaim your presence; it speaks for itself. The real question then is, does your presence in the face of others align with your essence? That is, does your leadership presence align with the perception of who you are as a leader? Understand that your staff are never following who you claim to be as a leader. They are always following their perception of who you are. Their perception of who you are is always rooted in what your presence represents to them.

> *Protection Pointer.* You may have convinced yourself that what defines your leadership is who you are as an instructional leader. In your mind, you are all about

instructional leadership. You are convinced that your presence represents instructional leadership. But when your staff are surveyed, they have a very different perception of you (e.g., to several of them, your presence represents discipline, to others inapproachability, to yet others difficult to talk to and out of touch). If you started out as a strong instructional leader but devolved into being, for example, inapproachable, your presence has been compromised. You didn't protect it, and now, in the eyes of your staff, you are someone other than who you were initially. If instructional leadership is important to you such that you contend that it is significant to student progress and achievement, then you must diligently ensure that you continue to perform as an instructional leader and be seen as one by your staff to protect your presence as an instructional leader.

Q26 How am I protecting my leadership values?

I previously discussed leadership presence and stated that I wanted my leadership presence to represent excellence. I want to build on that by discussing leadership values. As a leader, I had certain values that I would under no circumstances allow to be compromised. Therefore, I had to protect them at all cost. An example of this would be during my second month as an assistant principal in February 1998. It was Black History Month, and we had an assembly in honor of it.

Looking Back: The song "Lift Every Voice and Sing"—universally considered the Black national anthem—is a sacred song within the African American community and widely sung to commence a variety of programs that involve African Americans. When the staff and students were asked to stand for the singing of the anthem, there was a loud "Aww" from the students. Although I was only one month into my assistant principalship, I could not and would not allow that to go unaddressed. Before the pianist started to play, I had everyone sit down. I explained the historical significance of the song and asked the students to stand again. Although I didn't require that they all sing, I required that they respect the song via the elimination of the "Aww." After about three attempts, there was complete silence and we sang the anthem.

"Lift Every Voice and Sing" sung in a school (or any public venue) devoid of respect for it is a value of mine that I will not allow to be compromised. Countless times in my capacity as a public speaker, the song was received in the same manner at student assemblies where I was the speaker, and my response was exactly the same. I will not allow my leadership values, in this case as they relate to the disrespect of this song, to be compromised. I will protect my leadership values so that, ultimately, they become a part of my leadership presence.

What about *you*?

What are your leadership values? Have you considered what your leadership values are? Are your leadership values evident to your staff and students? Do you lead within your leadership values? Would you allow any of your leadership values to be compromised under certain circumstances? What do you do to protect your values in situations where they are being called into question? At the proverbial end of the day, your values are the foundation upon which you stand. They define who you are and what you are about. To compromise your values is essentially compromising yourself. Assuming that your administrative journey is a long one, I am certain that there will be times when you are going to have to make a decision that may result in your values being called into question or conflicting with the status quo or potentially being compromised. What are you going to do? The answer is personal, but I raise the question here because it, too, is a part of leadership.

I led four schools in my 14-year school leadership career. I once led a school where my values were severely called into question. It boiled down to me either acquiescing and submitting to something that went against everything I stood for or leaving the school. I stayed for the remainder of the year because I did not want to abandon my students mid-year, and I resigned at the end of the school year. I went on to a school where my values were respected and appreciated. Your values are your essence, and you must protect them.

Q27 How am I protecting my leadership open-mindedness?

When I became an administrator, student fashion did not include blue jeans with holes in the thighs. During my years as a high school principal, I started to notice a new trend with jeans where slowly but surely, they started to contain small holes. As time progressed, the holes started getting larger. Although my district had a student dress policy, it did not address holes in jeans because this was a new phenomenon. Additionally, I did not require that students wear uniforms. Another value of mine was that students be allowed to express their individuality through their attire as long as it met the requirements of the district dress policy. As I continued to see more and more students coming to school with holes in their jeans, I finally decided that it was time to address my students about them. I had the entire school report to the gym on a Thursday and, in a nutshell, told them I was banning jeans with holes effective the following Monday. On Thursday evening, I received a lengthy email from one of my seniors, who stated that he was writing on behalf of the entire school. He brought to my attention the fact that in the neighborhoods where the students shop, that style of jeans was all that the stores sold. He also informed me that it would be difficult for the students to shop for jeans so late in the year and that jeans can be expensive for them. I read the email several times while putting myself in the shoes of my students. I concluded that I had rushed to judgment and made my decision without thinking it through or engaging with my students. I did not give them a voice in that moment. I called my students together the next day and brought the author of the email to the front with me. I spoke highly of him and told my students that as a result of his email, I would permit students to wear jeans with the smaller holes. They understood. I also allowed the student who wrote the email to address his peers, who applauded him loudly.

I have always prided myself on having an open mind and here, my open-mindedness was being tested. Instead of dismissing my student's appeal, I listened, learned, and moved in an unintended direction. I didn't allow my open-mindedness to be compromised. I protected it and it was more than evident that the respect that my students had for me increased because I respected their collective voice.

What about *you*?

Do you lead with an open mind? Are you open to listening to the ideas, recommendations, and suggestions of your staff and students? Have you played a role in creating a culture where the ideas, recommendations, and suggestions of staff and students are welcomed? Have you created an environment where your students and staff feel comfortable approaching you with ideas, recommendations, and suggestions? Or is the culture in the building such that the students and staff feel intimidated about approaching you or that their ideas will not be taken seriously or go unheard? These are important questions to consider about yourself and your leadership.

As an assistant principal, you will be required to make count-less on-the-spot decisions that you will have to live with. You won't always have the time to think your decisions through. What's key is that you always allow yourself to keep an open mind when you make decisions. There is so much human cap-ital among your staff and students, who have myriad perspec-tives and experiences. Although you cannot lean on every staff person for every decision, there are people in your building you can lean on when you have some tough decisions to make. At those times, I encourage you to have an open mind and refrain from feeling that because you are either an assistant principal or principal you cannot consider the perspectives of those in your building who serve in non-administrative capacities. You must protect your open-mindedness while being willing to listen to the points of view of others.

Q28 How am I protecting my leadership influence?

When I became a teacher, an assistant principal, and a principal, I was extremely clear as to why I chose to hold those titles. I knew precisely what I wanted to accomplish and it was all rooted, as I stated earlier, in Black male empowerment. I wanted to prove to the world what my Black male learners were capable of achieving when in an environment that was conducive to their being willing to strive to maximize their potential. I knew that the environment—the climate, the culture, the educators, and leadership—was a key component. What simultaneously surprised me and brought me joy was the volume of my boys' mothers who informed me that their sons regularly talked about me and would sometimes talk like me, use my phrases and clichés—and the younger ones would even walk like me. This spoke volumes about the influence I had on my young men. I positioned myself in their lives in such a way that they were inspired by me, liked me, and wanted to be like me. I knew what I wanted to accomplish, but I had no idea it would translate to this level of influence. What was key, though, was that I had to protect my influence. Although I was always being my authentic self, if I let my guard down so to speak, the students could potentially see me in an unintended light. Because I knew that the children were learning from me and watching me, I had to be forever conscious of this reality because I never wanted to disappoint them relative to how they looked up to me and the influence that I had on them. I could never allow that to be compromised. It had to be protected via my consistent effort to always remain my authentic self in the classroom and as a school leader.

What about *you*?

Typically, when I think of the word "influence," I think of the word "control." Influence is the *capacity* to have an effect on the character, development, or behavior of someone or something. Control is the *power* to influence or direct people's behavior or course of events. As it related to my staff and students, I understood the need to be in control of certain situations from a managerial/leadership standpoint. But as it relates to the overall culture of the school, influence matters most. You will not achieve optimal results if it is solely your title that moves people to action. But on the other hand, when staff and students are moved to act because of your character and what you represent as a person and a leader, there is a much higher probability that your school will soar. Control is essentially making people act. Influence inspires them to act.

As a school leader, on what aspects of your students' lives do you have influence? On what aspects of your teachers' pedagogy do you have influence? Are you able to conclude that you have influence over the classroom experience of your students? Is there something about your presence in your school that has influence over the probability for the success of your students? Does your leadership influence the academic, social, and emotional growth and development of your students? In what ways does your leadership influence the recognition of the individuality of each of the learners in your school? In what ways does your leadership influence the recognition of the cultural identity of each of the learners in your school? In what ways does your leadership influence the recognition of the voice of each of the learners in your school? How does your leadership influence your school's brand identity? How does your leadership influence your school's mission and vision? How does your leadership influence your school's climate and culture? How does your leadership influence the social-emotional needs of your students? How does your leadership influence the academic performance of your students?

As you consider your influence in a wide array of areas relative to the aforementioned questions, and as you establish your influence, always remember that it must also be protected. Compromise of your influence can translate to a compromise of your credibility as a leader. You must strive to maintain a high level of consistency within the influential leader you have crafted yourself to be.

Q29 How am I protecting my leadership decisiveness?

During my 14 years in school leadership, I had eight superintendents. I have always been one who followed all directives and complied with all of the expectations of the district for which I worked. That is, I could be counted on to lead within the guidelines and expectations of the district. It doesn't mean I didn't challenge or question a decision behind closed doors. But after my concern had been raised and discussed, I complied—with one exception. I had a superintendent who had an extended-day initiative that would have had middle-school-aged children walking home after dark. I challenged the decision because I vehemently felt it made for a very long day for children and that walking home in the dark was not safe. I was also mindful of the numerous students who were engaged in extracurricular activities and those who were picking up and watching over younger siblings at home. The parents agreed with me, but the superintendent was adamant. I explained to him that the parents informed me that they were not going to go for it. My superintendent ordered me not to let the students leave the building at dismissal and to have my security officers stationed at all of the exit doors to prevent them from leaving. Let that one marinate for a moment.

That one time in my career, I defied a directive and it almost cost me my job, my reputation, and my career. It was a dark period in my life professionally and personally, but I got through it, and five years later received the prestigious Milken Educator Award (for my work as a leader in a different district). My point is I made a decision, stood by it, and was and continue to be proud of it. I did not waver from my decision even though I knew that I could possibly lose everything I'd worked so hard for years to attain. As I look back on it 20 years later, I remain proud of my decision. All of those children are adults now, and many of them are connected to me on social media. I would not be able to handle one of them saying to me, "I still remember when you kept us from leaving school by having security prevent us from leaving after school hours." I made a decision on principle and let the chips fall where they may. I did not compromise my principles and values so that life would be OK for me professionally and personally. Instead, I protected my principles and values. Moreover, I didn't compromise my decisiveness as a leader. I made a decision, and I stood by it.

What about *you*?

I am well aware that the aforementioned scenario was an extreme situation, but I wanted to present it to highlight the significance of protecting your leadership decisiveness. It is my hope that you never find yourself in a situation where you have to make a tough decision that results in having to choose between your principles or values and job or career, but they do arise from time to time.

In your current assistant principal capacity, are you one who makes a lot of decisions during the day? Are you required to consult with your principal before you make decisions? Are you one who feels the need to have staff approve your decisions? Does your desire to be liked by staff drive your decision making? Are you able to own up to a bad decision that you made?

You chose leadership. Many of you who are reading this book aspire to become principals, which will probably require more decision making than you ever experienced in your life. Throughout the day, you are making decisions—in some cases, life-altering ones. As a decision maker, you will sometimes have the time and ability to survey the various groups for whom you are making decisions (e.g., students and staff). But that won't be your norm. As a leader, you will frequently have to make split-second decisions that may have far-reaching implications. You won't always have time to consult with others. In fact, there will be times when you have to make a quick decision that no one agrees with, but it'll be your decision nevertheless. And because you made the decision, you will have to stand by it . . . alone. So as I say to many newer leaders, you can't be one who *needs* to be *loved* by everyone. If the only decisions you can make are the ones that everyone is on board with and will praise you for, *you are in the wrong business.* As a leader, you must be decisive in your decision making. When you allow your decisiveness in making decisions to be compromised, you have essentially sabotaged your leadership authority because every- one in the building will see that the decisions that you make can be compromised in any given situation. Once you make a decision, even if it's an unpopular one, you must hold firm and protect it.

Let me remind you that not all decisions are going to be good or the best ones possible. Therefore, before you make them, think them through as best and as quickly as you can. But know that when you make a bad decision, it is not a bad thing to own up to it and reverse it. That's leadership too. It just can't become habitual because if it does, that becomes your reputation as a leader, and your downfall is impending.

Q30 How am I protecting my leadership reliability/dependability?

After my first week as the new assistant principal, my principal left the school for a weeklong conference. My tenure as an assistant principal commenced in January that year, so we're talking about a middle school of 650 students and their teachers who were very accustomed to the ways and leadership in place before I arrived. When my principal left for his conference, he essentially handed me the keys for one week after having had only one week of experience as an assistant principal. I didn't have an administrator to assist me. I was all alone. I was excited and desperately wanted to prove to my principal, our staff and students, and myself that I was more than capable of holding it together, of leading effectively. I wanted to prove to my principal that I was reliable. I wanted him to be able to leave the building and be confident that the school was in good hands. Reflecting on it now, I have no regrets about what was essentially my first opportunity to lead a school as an acting principal.

Through the remainder of my assistant principalship, I often served in an acting principal capacity. I continued to want to demonstrate to my principal that he could rely on me to lead effectively. I wanted to be perceived as dependable. In striving to be effective in my principal's absence, I was protecting my leadership reliability, which was extremely important to me as a new leader. And I indeed passed the test. My principal felt that I always did a fine job in his absence.

What about *you*?

Can your principal rely on you in their absence? Can your principal rely on you for a wide variety of aspects of school leadership? Can your principal rely on you to complement their leadership? Can your principal rely on you to have their back during challenging situations? Can the leadership team rely on you as a dependable team member? Can your students and staff rely on you in times of need? When you look at yourself in the mirror, does the person looking back feel that you are a reliable assistant principal in most, if not all, instances?

As an assistant principal, there will be many times when your principal has to leave the school for a variety of reasons. In some districts, the principal may frequently leave the building; depending upon how many assistant principals are in your building, that may be your opportunity to serve as acting principal. Your principal is going to be relying on you to make their absence seamless and as you continue to serve in this role, you must continue to strive to be the best version of yourself. In so doing, you are protecting your leadership reliability to the extent that your principal can always count on you to step in and lead in their absence.

In addition to your principal leaving the building, there are countless other scenarios where your principal and others in the building will rely on your leadership effectiveness. You must make it a priority to be reliable in all of your leadership endeavors. Your students, staff, and the leadership team must know that you are a leader who can be relied upon and depended on in a variety of situations. That's in part how trust and confidence are established between administration and staff. What's key is your consistency. Your consistency matters in your leadership and must be protected. Compromising your reliability between your leadership and staff or your leadership and your principal can compromise the trust that both parties have in you and your leadership.

Q31 How am I protecting my leadership durability?

In the sports world, they say the best ability is availability. That is, due to the inevitability of injuries in sports, many athletes are simply not available. On the other hand, there are athletes who have a superior training and conditioning regimen during both the season and the off-season that exponentially reduces the risk of injury. Some of them invest hundreds of thousands of dollars in their bodies toward extending their careers and keeping themselves available. These are what you call durable athletes.

The world of school leadership requires durability as well.

> *Looking Back:* On May 1, 2015, I suffered a heart attack while delivering a keynote address in Miami, Florida. There were no warning signs, and up to the point of the heart attack, I felt absolutely great. The day after, the

doctors informed me that I had a 100 percent plaque buildup in my main artery; it caused the heart attack and could have caused my demise. I also learned that my heart attack was fully preventable. My horrible fast-food diet, which worsened when I became a school adminis- trator, was off the charts by the time I became a full-time speaker/consultant and was literally killing me slowly. I lived on that diet while on the road and on that fateful day, it almost took me out. I was sidelined for a period, and I had to cancel some engagements. I was no longer available. Through lack of an exercise regimen and a very poor diet, I compromised my durability while leaving it unprotected. My mental health was affected as well. I didn't share with anyone (not even with those closest to me) that I was in a state of depression/not well mentally and emotionally.

I eventually recovered. My diet shifted dramatically, I exercise for about 45 minutes five days per week at a minimum, and I began to open up to the people who mattered most to me. I have a cardio regimen that has me feeling quite well physically and emotionally, and along with my improved diet, I'm keeping a whole lot of the old weight off. I now feel stronger than I ever did. With the brutal travel and speaking schedule that I have, I cannot afford to cut corners on my health. It has been eight years since my heart attack, and I feel great.

What about *you*?

How are you protecting your durability? What measures are you taking to sustain good health? Do you have an exercise regimen? Do you maintain a healthy diet? What are you doing for your mental health? Are your physical and mental health priorities of your leadership? Do you ever find yourself cutting corners on your physical and mental health (both of which play significant roles relative to how you sustain your leadership durability)?

Leadership is by no stretch of the imagination a sprint. It is a marathon. And just as a marathon runner has to have great durability and endurance, so does a school leader. As a school leader, you are being pulled in more directions than you probably ever imagined before you took on your first assignment; this can be quite overwhelming physically, emotionally, psychologically, and spiritually. In school leadership, the expectation that you be proficient and effective in a variety of areas is just the reality of being a school leader. But one of those areas of leadership that can never be ignored is how you delegate responsibility, empower others, and use the human capital around you. This goes a long way toward increasing your durability. You cannot do this work alone. It will burn you out quickly. The goal must always be to create synergy, which in turn is protecting your leadership durability.

Additionally, your diet and exercise regimen matter. Toward attaining longevity as a leader, your body matters. What you put into your body matters. As they say, "you are what you eat." How you treat your body matters. Be sure to protect your leadership durability by protecting your body at all costs.

Q32 How am I protecting my leadership integrity?

I once had a superintendent who regularly said to principals at our administrators' meeting that "sex, money, drugs, and sports" can be our downfall if we are not mindful of the implications of each on all levels and all aspects of our leadership. Every time he uttered those words, they resonated with me—particularly the money and sports.

In the second half of my leadership career, I became a high school principal and I was introduced at that juncture to the world of varsity athletics. There was so much that I thought I knew but in actuality didn't know at all. I did not understand at the time that varsity athletics was a big business and that many competing interests were involved relative to acquiring superior athletes and winning. This was definitely not the elementary school program. As the principal, I had to ensure that all i's were dotted and all t's were crossed. Making bad decisions relative to my student athletes in the name of winning could have spelled my demise as a leader. My integrity as the leader of the school had to mean more to me than winning games. I could not allow it to be compromised.

On the other hand, I was around thousands more dollars, both physical and electronic, than I'd been at the elementary and middle school levels. I was never tempted to steal money, but it would have been extremely easy to do so. This is once again where your integrity must kick in. This is where your ethics—doing the right thing when no one is watching—must kick in. My integrity allowed me to always do the right thing with the funds we collected and with the money in my budget. My integrity allowed me to sleep well at night.

What about *you*?

What might your students say about your integrity? What might your staff say about your integrity? When you look into your mirror, who do you see regarding your integrity? Are you able to always do the right thing when no one is watching? Does the way that you are being perceived matter to you? Countless school leaders over the years have made bad decisions regarding money. The consequences were harsh (arrests, terminations, and revocations of licenses to lead) and their integrity and thereby their reputations were compromised, perhaps permanently. (A simple Google search will reveal an endless stream of school leadership financial dishonesty.)

This work is not for you if you do not possess integrity in all aspects of your leadership. There's no place in school leadership for a dishonest, unethical leader. As a principal and even an assistant principal, you will be in contact with a lot of cash throughout your career. You must be ever so cognizant of the fact that the money does not belong to you—not one cent of it. There are policies, codes, and statutes that govern how you use money associated with your school and district. Just because you want to help a family in need, for example, doesn't mean you can use school funds for that purpose. Doing so would more than likely be breaking the law. And doing so would completely compromise your leadership integrity. And once your integrity is compromised, it can be rather difficult to restore it.

My message to you is to always do the right thing. Protect your leadership integrity. But always keep in mind, when I say the right thing, I am saying the right thing rooted in your district's policies and your state's codes and statutes, not in your emotions. Do you know your district's policies and your state's codes and statutes? Do you know them as if you wrote them? If not, I suggest you put this book down, pick them up and begin to study them, and then come back to this book.

Q33 How am I protecting my leadership trustworthiness?

Closely associated with your integrity is your trustworthiness.

July 1, 2003, was my first day back in my home district of East Orange, New Jersey, and I was excited about the prospects for the new school year in my new school in the city that raised me personally and professionally. On July 5, I received a letter from the New Jersey State Department of Education stating that my new school, along with six others, was on the persistently dangerous list under the No Child Left Behind law. (I vehemently disagree now and disagreed then with the school having been on that list. I knew the school from a distance, and I knew it wasn't a "dangerous" school.) Be that as it may, we were on the list and covered rather extensively and nationally by the media. Under No Child Left Behind, parents had the option of transferring their children to a school in the district that was considered safer. I was not standing for it and called a schoolwide parent meeting to assure the parents that their children would be safe and receive a world-class education. All parents decided to opt in with the exception of one (who later asked to be reinstated within a month of leaving my school).

I will never forget the response to a question posed to a parent during a television interview (that I still watch) with some of the parents from my school. She looked into the camera and said, "Mr. Kafele told us to trust him, and we do." Her words resonated with me—then and always. I had to deliver based on their trust and, according to the parents, I did. I refused to violate the trust that the parents had in me, which was rooted in the parent–community conversation I had with them that summer. I knew that my word was my bond, and I wasn't going to compromise their trust in me. I was going to protect it with every fiber of my being to sustain the trustworthiness that the parents had in me from Day 1.

What about *you*?

Do your students, staff, and principal consider you to be trustworthy? In your leadership capacity, have you ever made a promise that you couldn't deliver on? If so, how did you save face in that situation? How did you grow in that situation? How did you go about regaining the trust of those affected? Like integrity, trust is extremely fragile. You can be trusted one day and looked upon suspiciously the next. If you make a promise, keep it. If you can't keep a promise in a given situation, don't make one. No one wants to hear excuses. If you are not sure that you can deliver on a promise, don't make the promise because once the promise is made, you are going to be held accountable by whomever you made the promise to. When you fail to deliver and particularly if you demonstrate a pattern of inconsistency, regaining their trust will be virtually impossible.

In the above scenario, I felt very confident and comfortable proclaiming that we would be alright and removed from the persistently dangerous list. I had been a principal for four years by then and was confident in my skill set. At the end of that year, I was informed by the State Department of Education that we had been removed from the list. I delivered. To all of the assistant principals reading this book, do not make promises that you cannot keep. I repeat: Do not make promises that you cannot keep. When you do, your trustworthiness is on the line and is being tested. You never, ever want to put your trustworthiness in jeopardy. You never, ever want to compromise your trustworthiness. You must protect it with everything that you have. And you do this by delivering on *every* promise that you make.

Q34 How am I protecting my leadership *character?*

I have always prided myself on having a character that was warm and courteous and empathetic. It was never about me but always about the people around me . . . the people I led. It was always about being a humble servant—buying lunches for students, taking students to a restaurant for dinner, buying clothes for students, helping out a parent or staff member with the rent, offering scholarships out of my pocket, taking my entire junior class to Six Flags with my Milken Educator Award winnings, taking a student off of the streets, visiting homes after hours, speaking at funerals, and so on. It was all about my students, staff, parents, and the school community. But, equally important, it was all about my character. As I reflect on it in real time as I type, my behavior toward the aforementioned stakeholders was not something that I had to create or develop. It was who I was as a man, and it carried over into my leadership. It was my character that made me an ideal fit for the populations that I served. But although my character was me, I still had to be vigilant toward preventing my character from being compromised. When one's character is compromised, it is very difficult to redeem oneself. Now that all of my former students are adults, I could run into any of them virtually anywhere. Just that alone makes me ever so cautious of my public behavior. I don't ever want to run into a former student and feel a sense of embarrassment. Therefore, I protect my character always, just as I did when I was a principal and an assistant principal. I made sure that my public behavior and school behavior were consistent with my character.

What about *you*?

I cannot overstate the significance of your character in the eyes of your students, staff, parents, community, and even central office staff. Your character addresses who you are beyond who you claim to be. I tell people all the time, you can only hide from yourself for so long. Eventually, the real you is going to emerge. For example, a huge number of job seekers for teaching, assistant principal, and principal positions reach out to me regularly to inquire about what their portfolios should contain. I tell them all the time that I personally have no use for a portfolio. I instead want to have a long conversation with the candidate. That candidate can put on a show all they want. Through my questioning during that long conversation, if they initially suppressed their true self, eventually who they are—their character—is going to emerge.

As an assistant principal, your character matters. Your character is who everyone else sees. Is what they see consistent with who you claim to be? Is what they see who you think you are? Is what they see an exact representation of who you are? Is what they see someone you can be proud of at the end of the day? Is what they see what you would one day train an assistant principal to become? Is what they see the same person who was hungry for leadership success in graduate school? Is what they see the same person who interviewed for your current position? Is what they see the same person you are when you are in the presence of your immediate supervisor? These questions matter as you strive to never compromise your character to protect it by being the leader that you know your constituents deserve.

Q35 How am I protecting my leadership *smile?*

I am ending this first volume of *The Assistant Principal Identity* with a twist. I am simply reminding you to smile. This work can be so overwhelming that we can often forget to smile. During my first few years in assistant principal and principal leadership, my students would literally ask me why I never smiled. In my mind, I was smiling all the time. But, as it turned out, I wasn't. This, too, I worked on because as I gained experience and wisdom as a leader, I learned that I can smile and maintain my authority as the leader. Smiling was not a sign of weakness as some believe. Smiling became a sign of compassion for my students, staff, and the overall school. Smiling, as opposed to looking angry all the time, endeared me to my students. Smiling helped me to become a much better leader, particularly relative to building relationships.

What about *you?*

Do your students and staff get to see you smile? Are you under the impression that smiling is a sign of weakness? Do you feel that you have a reason to smile in your school? Do you feel that there aren't a lot of reasons to smile in your school? Would smiling change the way you are perceived by your students and staff? If so, how? If not, why not?

There are a plethora of challenges and obstacles on any given day of the week in school buildings. I don't think anyone would argue with that. But for some of those challenges, we may be looking in the wrong direction for solutions. Sometimes, the answer is simply in a smile. A child may enter school extremely down about something that occurred at home. And because of the emotion that the incident engendered, the child may be on the brink of an outburst or a meltdown. But then, there's you. You have established a rapport with this youngster. You have credibility in her eyes. You greet her with a warm smile, and it opens the door to a dialogue. In other words, a smile can go a long way. It, too, must be protected through your diligence. Always remember that you are leading human beings who have real human emotions and that sometimes a smile from you might be all they need.

Conclusion

Conclusion

As you see, I did something a little different with this book. The focus wasn't solely on growing and developing in certain areas. Rather, it was on protecting what you have in the same way that you protect your loved ones and belongings. My intent for this book was for you to closely examine your leadership mindset, fervor, and authenticity while taking a close look at the areas that may have been unintentionally compromised and determining what you need to do to restore them and ultimately protect them. The protection of leadership mindset, fervor, and authenticity truly matters.

To illustrate my point, recently, as I was rushing through an airport to catch my flight, I passed a men's clothing store with several pairs of shoes on display at the front entrance. One pair of shoes—shiny burgundy wingtips—instantly caught my attention. They had my name on them. I knew that I had to board my flight in 10 minutes and was a 10-minute walk away from the gate, but I wanted those shoes! I tried them on quickly; they looked and felt great, and I knew walking onto a stage with them on would give me a look that I'd never had before. I paid for them and threw them into my carry-on bag and dashed to my gate. I was going to wear them at the next morning's presentation.

When I arrived at my hotel and took the shoes out of my bag, it dawned upon me that I couldn't wear them the next day—as I don't wear unpolished shoes. I treasure all of my shoes. I value all of my shoes. I take good care of all of my shoes. I protect my shoes from the elements and potential scuffs. Rather than risk damaging them, I didn't wear them.

This is what I mean when I say that protecting your leadership mindset, fervor, and authenticity truly matters; it's critical to your success. You must treasure, value, and take as good care of them as I do with my shoes. You cannot and you must not *ever* walk into your school with them unprotected. There's too much at stake in these most critical times. Failure to protect your leadership mindset, fervor, and authenticity can compromise your overall leadership effectiveness, and when that happens, everyone suffers.

You got this now, so let's go!

Bibliography

Kafele, B. K. (2009). *Motivating Black males to achieve in school and in life.* ASCD.

Kafele, B. (2013). *Closing the attitude gap: How to fire up your students to strive for success.* ASCD.

Kafele, B. K. (2016). *The teacher 50: Critical questions for inspiring classroom excellence.* ASCD.

Kafele, B. K. (2019, July 1). The assistant principalship: The most misunderstood and underutilized position in education. *Principal Kafele Writes.* http://www.principalkafelewrites.com/2019/07/the-assistant-principalship-most.html

Kafele, B. K. (2019). *Is my school a better school because I lead it?* ASCD.

Kafele, B. K. (2020). *The assistant principal 50: Critical questions for meaningful leadership and professional growth.* ASCD.

Kafele, B. K. (2021, November 7). Equity is not a "four-letter word," the "boogey man," a political statement, nor the enemy . . . IT'S JUST GREAT TEACHING! *Principal Kafele Writes.* http://www.principalkafelewrites.com/2021/11/equity-is-not-four-letter-word-boogey.html

Kafele, B. K. (2021). *The equity and social justice education 50: Critical questions for improving opportunities and outcomes for Black students.* ASCD.

Lopez, N. (2016). *The bridge to brilliance: How one principal in a tough community is inspiring the world.* Viking.

Muhammad, A. (2009). *Transforming school culture: How to overcome staff division.* Solution Tree.

Schwanke, J. (2016). *You're the principal! Now what? Strategies and solutions for new school leaders.* ASCD.

Sterrett, W. (2011). *Insights into action: Successful school leaders share what works.* ASCD.

Thomas-EL, S., Jones, J., & Vari, T. J. (2020). *Passionate leadership: Creating a culture of success in every school.* Corwin.

Whitaker, T. (2003). *What great principals do differently.* Eye on Education.

Index

About the Author

**B**aruti K. Kafele, a highly regarded urban educator in New Jersey for more than 20 years, has distinguished himself as a master teacher and a transformational school leader. As an elementary school teacher in East Orange, New Jersey, he was named East Orange School District and Essex County Public Schools Teacher of the Year, and he was a finalist for New Jersey State Teacher of the Year. As a middle and high school principal, he led the transformation of four different New Jersey urban schools, including Newark Tech, which went from a low-performing school in need of improvement to national recognition, and which was recognized by *U.S. News & World Report* as one of America's best high schools.

Kafele is one of the most sought-after school leadership experts in North America. He is the author of 13 books, including the ASCD book *The Aspiring Principal 50* and his seven ASCD bestsellers—*The Assistant Principal 50*, *Closing the Attitude Gap*, *The Equity and Social Justice Education 50*, *Is My School a Better School Because I Lead It?*, *Motivating Black Males to Achieve in School and in Life*, *The Principal 50*, and *The Teacher 50*. He is the recipient of more than 150 educational, professional, and community awards, including the prestigious Milken Educator Award and the National Alliance of Black School Educators Hall of Fame Award. He was inducted into the East Orange, New Jersey, Hall of Fame, and the city of Dickinson, Texas, proclaimed February 8, 1998, Baruti Kafele Day. Kafele can be reached via his website, www.principalkafele.com.

Related ASCD Resources: Leadership

At the time of publication, the following resources were available (ASCD stock numbers in parentheses).

The Aspiring Principal 50: Critical Questions for New and Future School Leaders by Baruti K. Kafele (#120023)

The Assistant Principal 50: Critical Questions for Meaningful Leadership and Professional Growth by Baruti K. Kafele (#121018)

Balanced Leadership for Powerful Learning: Tools for Achieving Success in Your School by Bryan Goodwin & Greg Cameron with Heather Hein (#112025)

Creating a Culture of Reflective Practice: Capacity-Building for Schoolwide Success by Pete Hall & Alisa Simeral (#117006)

Educator Bandwidth: How to Reclaim Your Energy, Passion, and Time by Jane Kise & Ann Holm (#122019)

Is My School a Better School Because I Lead It? by Baruti K. Kafele (#120013)

Leading with Focus: Elevating the Essentials for School and District Improvement by Mike Schmoker (#116024)

The Principal as Chief Empathy Officer: Creating a Culture Where Everyone Grows by Thomas R. Hoerr (#122030)

The Principal 50: Critical Leadership Questions for Inspiring Schoolwide Excellence by Baruti K. Kafele (#115050)

Qualities of Effective Principals, 2nd Edition by James H. Stronge & Xianxuan Xu (#121022)

What's Your Leadership Story? A School Leader's Guide to Aligning How You Lead with Who You Are by Gretchen Oltman & Vicki Bautista (#121020)

You're the Principal! Now What? Strategies and Solutions for New School Leaders by Jen Schwanke (#117003)

For up-to-date information about ASCD resources, go to **www.ascd.org**. You can search the complete archives of *Educational Leadership* at **www.ascd.org/el**. To contact us, send an email to member@ascd.org or call 1-800-933-2723 or 703-578-9600.

ascd
whole child

The ASCD Whole Child approach is an effort to transition from a focus on narrowly defined academic achievement to one that promotes the long-term development and success of all children. Through this approach, ASCD supports educators, families, community members, and policymakers as they move from a vision about educating the whole child to sustainable, collaborative actions.

The Assistant Principal Identity relates to the **supported** tenet. *For more about the ASCD Whole Child approach, visit* **www.ascd.org/wholechild.**

WHOLE CHILD
TENETS

1 HEALTHY
Each student enters school healthy and learns about and practices a healthy lifestyle.

2 SAFE
Each student learns in an environment that is physically and emotionally safe for students and adults.

3 ENGAGED
Each student is actively engaged in learning and is connected to the school and broader community.

4 SUPPORTED
Each student has access to personalized learning and is supported by qualified, caring adults.

5 CHALLENGED
Each student is challenged academically and prepared for success in college or further study and for employment and participation in a global environment.